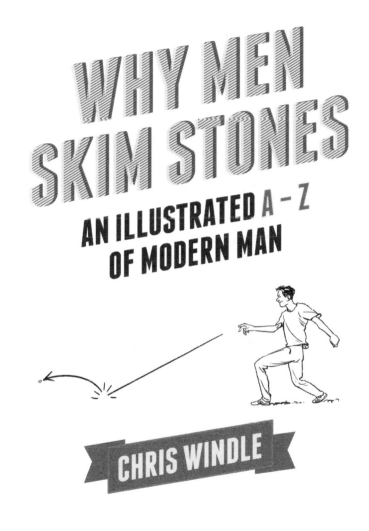

WHY MEN SKIM STONES

AN ILLUSTRATED A–Z OF MODERN MAN

CHRIS WINDLE

◨ SQUARE PEG

1 3 5 7 9 10 8 6 4 2

Square Peg, an imprint of Vintage,
20 Vauxhall Bridge Road,
London SW1V 2SA

Square Peg is part of the Penguin Random House
group of companies whose addresses can be found at
global.penguinrandomhouse.com.

Copyright © Chris Windle 2015

Illustrations by Quinton Winter © Square Peg 2015

Chris Windle has asserted his right to be identified as the author
of this Work in accordance with the Copyright, Designs and
Patents Act 1988

First published by Square Peg in 2015

www.vintage-books.co.uk

A CIP catalogue record for this book is available
from the British Library

ISBN 9780224101004

Printed and bound by TJ International
Designed by carrdesignstudio.com

Penguin Random House is committed to a sustainable future for our
business, our readers and our planet. This book is made from Forest
Stewardship Council® certified paper.

Introduction

Have you ever watched a man and wondered: 'what is he doing?' If the answer to that is, as it must be: 'yes', then you've come to the right book.

When Shakespeare wrote: 'The fool doth think he is wise, but the wise man knows himself to be a fool', he was articulating the fact that most men are idiots in one way or another. Indeed, he probably jotted the line down after witnessing a man arguing with an inanimate object, pretending to swallow an item of cutlery, or attempting to eat a 3ft-wide burger.

Many of man's oddest habits have become such an integral part of the male identity that society has stopped seeking explanations. But, finally, here is a book that allows you to delve into the male brain without having to perform a messy operation. A book that sheds light on why he spends so much more time thinking about a zombie apocalypse than is strictly necessary considering the likelihood of one occurring.

Also included are handy guides designed to help men triumph in situations they may sometimes find difficult, such as: How to bleed a radiator, How to catch a spider and How to hold a newborn baby. Because men love to have a set of instructions on hand that they can steadfastly ignore until everything goes wrong.

Of course, the bizarre traits documented here aren't limited to men – plenty of women air drum and devote countless hours to watching documentaries about sharks, too – but through sheer weight of numbers and an acute susceptibility to stupidity, men have made such behavioural patterns their own.

Some men will laugh and think: 'Ha, that's not me' – just before practising a forward defensive prod with an imaginary cricket bat. Some may find solace in the fact they are not alone, and may even begin to feel a little pride in these shared quirks.

For female readers, this book will promote a greater understanding of that most misunderstood of creatures: modern man. Even as he engages in yet another pointless, perhaps downright dangerous, pursuit.

A
is for ...

Adjusting things

No picture, even a perfectly straight one, is perfectly straight until a man has adjusted it. Only once he has placed a hand on each side of the frame and given it the benefit of his internal spirit level, by carefully tilting it one way and then the other, does he trust it is in perfect alignment. You may notice your picture is subsequently slightly askew.

This also applies to mirrors, coat rails and shelves.

Agreeing when he disagrees

A man would rather hand over good money for a carpet he hates than prolong the carpet-shopping experience. Likewise curtains and crockery.

Air drumming

The air drum is the superior cousin of the air guitar. An imaginary Fender offers far less freedom than two pretend sticks and the biggest drum kit a brain can conceive of. What's more, the air drum may be played on a steering wheel while driving, although the artiste should be careful not to press too hard on the foot drum when in built-up areas.

Because the air drum is a more expressive imaginary musical instrument, it allows the drummer to appreciate a song on a more profound level than the average air guitarist, who's just out for some fun. This panders to the male desire to prove that he 'gets it' more than the average Joe and so operates on a higher intellectual plane. This desire invariably ends up with him looking like an idiot.

If you ever spot a man silently flailing his arms around in a wild, rhythmic fashion while tilting his head forward, squeezing his eyes shut and gritting his teeth, leave him to it. He could be in the middle of his favourite percussion solo. Of course, there's also a chance he's about to go on a bloody rampage.

Airport drinking

There is only one place you can have a pint of lager for breakfast without raising concerns about your drinking habits. And that's the airport.

Normal rules don't apply once you're in the departure lounge. Time loses its meaning – after all, even if you've just woken up, it might be pub o'clock wherever you're travelling to.

'It seems, in fact, as though the second half of a man's life is made up of nothing but the habits he has accumulated during the first half.'

Fyodor Dostoevsky

Alphabetising CDs

A man often confuses 'cleaning' with 'rearranging his stuff'; that's why when you ask him to do the housework you might find him, hours later, surrounded by compact disc cases and listening to Meat Loaf.

Your first question will be either: 'Why didn't you start with the toilet?' or 'Why do you still own these when we threw away our CD player four years ago?' Obviously, if it was vinyl it would be different. Vinyl isn't meant to be played, it's there to give the impression he might once have been a DJ.

When domestic chores are in the offing a man will attempt to come up with a job that appears to be useful but is in fact a cover for doing something he enjoys. Reordering CDs isn't about 'improving the space-to-clutter ratio of the room', as he insists, it's about reacquainting himself with the Smiths album that soundtracked his first kiss with Rebecca Hathlethwaite in year 10.

Angling

Many men find sitting in the rain holding a stick preferable to sitting at home surrounded by central heating and a roof. This may seem odd to the casual observer.

Angling is a pastime that pits man against nature in a fierce tussle for survival, allowing him to take a seat and work his way through a large bag of pickled onion Monster Munch while he's at it. This combines the need to satisfy his prehistoric hunter-gatherer urge with a modern liking for inertia and overeating, making it a near perfect male hobby.

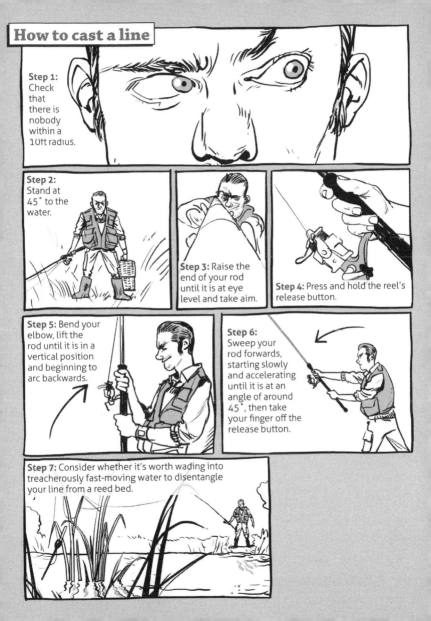

How to cast a line

Step 1: Check that there is nobody within a 10ft radius.

Step 2: Stand at 45° to the water.

Step 3: Raise the end of your rod until it is at eye level and take aim.

Step 4: Press and hold the reel's release button.

Step 5: Bend your elbow, lift the rod until it is in a vertical position and beginning to arc backwards.

Step 6: Sweep your rod forwards, starting slowly and accelerating until it is at an angle of around 45°, then take your finger off the release button.

Step 7: Consider whether it's worth wading into treacherously fast-moving water to disentangle your line from a reed bed.

Annoying each other

It is normal for younger male friends to act as if they actually hate each other. When they gather together you may notice them engaging in mutual light torture. This can include the repeated flicking of ears, the dangerous removal of seating and the addition of excessive chilli to foodstuffs.

In group situations men feel compelled to respond to such small-scale acts of social terrorism by repeating them. Only harder. Otherwise they might be deemed kind and sensitive. Eventually this culminates in everybody throwing pints over one another and, sometimes, a punch-up.

Arguing with inanimate objects

When a man walks into the corner of a table or struggles to open an over-stuffed cutlery drawer his natural instinct is to start angrily apportioning blame. If the answers to the questions: 'Who left that there?' and 'Who keeps putting the salad servers in here?' are 'him' and 'him', he will either accept the part he played in his own misfortune – unlikely – or shout obscenities at the object in question.

Similarly, if a man can't find his car keys or wallet he will growl accusingly at worktops, cupboards and the bowl he always leaves them in until he remembers where he actually left them.

(See also: Yelling at technology, page 224)

Arm-wrestling

When men go out together they have two communication settings: early evening small talk, usually involving sport; and late-night incoherent shouting, usually involving sport. To prevent the gap in between becoming a troubling silence, pierced only by the occasional crunch of a pork scratching – or to resolve a dispute involving sport – men will often resort to arm-wrestling.

It's an activity that sits nicely between a thumb war and full wrestling (see Wrestling old friends page 214), allowing a man to demonstrate his obscene strength while still holding a drink. It's also the only socially acceptable way for two men who aren't dating to hold hands. And all men want to hold hands really.

B

is for ...

Banter

Prevalent among groups of teenage boys, football commentators and men on stag dos, banter is the reciprocal exchange of witless remarks. The best banterers are those able to think of the least intelligent thing to say in the fastest time.

The banterer tends to describe any show of weakness – the inability to spend an entire day consuming nothing but sambuca and chips, for example – as 'gay', and regularly implies he has slept with his friends' mothers. This is particularly irritating if he has, in fact, slept with your mother.

Barbecuing

Men who show no interest in cooking within the confines of a kitchen are wont to spring out of their culinary torpor at the prospect of roasting raw animal flesh on the patio. It is a challenge their inner alpha male cannot resist, bearing little resemblance to the effete act of preparing food anybody actually wants to eat.

Partially concealed by smoke, sacrificing his lungs to provide sustenance for others, blinking away stinging charcoal fumes and wielding oversized utensils, in his mind he forms a heroic figure not far removed from the fireman who emerges blackened from a burning building clutching a crying baby. The only difference is that he will emerge clutching a plate of charred meat.

For the male who doesn't enjoy social occasions, manning the barbecue is also the perfect way to be present without actually having to talk to anybody for any length of time. You're far too busy; you've got some marinated chicken wings to turn!

How to barbecue meat using charcoal

Step 1: Shelter your barbecue from the wind so that it is easy to light and control.

Step 2: Build a charcoal pile in its centre and add firelighters at the base. Open your barbecue's vents and light the firelighters.

Step 3: Leave the charcoal to burn for around thirty minutes, or until most of it has turned white.

Step 4: Spread the hot charcoal using a suitable implement, ideally not the large fork you plan to cook with.

Step 5: Close the vents and place your meat at the centre of the grill, starting with the pieces most likely to cause food poisoning if undercooked. That's usually the chicken.

Step 6: Focus on cooking two types of meat properly. Just because you are barbecuing doesn't mean you have to cook an entire farmyard.

Step 7: Never prick sausages, just turn them regularly.

Step 8: A hood will help food cook faster and more evenly. If your barbecue has one move the meat to the edge of the grill and close the hood.

Step 9: Under a hood leave sausages for around five minutes, chicken for ten minutes and small whole joints for twenty minutes. If you do not have a hood make sure meat is browned all over and cooked through.

B

Step 10: When your guests have left, clean the grill. It is far better to do this straight away than to allow the grime to harden into a pork-based concrete.

Base jumping

One strange manifestation of the competitive male spirit is the relentless pursuit of bigger and better ways to endanger their own lives, such as base jumping. Its death-or-glory charms are particularly seductive to men with a taste for the spectacular and a blasé attitude to having their face scraped off a pavement, which is exactly what happened to pioneer base jumper Franz Reichelt when he leapt from the Eiffel Tower in 1912.

For this adrenaline-crazed bunch, skyscrapers are built with the specific purpose of providing a convenient spot to leap from when there aren't any mountains available.

It is one of the most dangerous recreational activities known to man, since base jumpers start off a lot closer to the ground than sky divers and don't attach themselves to an elasticated bungee rope, which to them is health and safety gone mad. Miscalculating when to open their parachutes is a mistake base jumpers regret for a very short time.

On the flip side, jumpers, especially those wearing a wing suit, briefly experience what it is like to be a bird. Albeit a bird that shouts 'awesome' a lot.

(See also: Bungee jumping, page 30)

Bear hugs

Unless two men meet in a professional context – and even then lines are blurred – a handshake is rarely enough. Men are now expected to wrap their arms around friends, friends of friends and distant acquaintances as if they are close family members.

The bear hug is designed to demonstrate a sense of camaraderie and affection without the emotional baggage that comes with a tender cuddle, which often leads to crying and the discussion of feelings. In the old days a tip of the hat and a 'good day, sir' did the same job.

Many men are rightfully frightened of the bear hug, which has the power to provoke an intense sense of awkwardness. This can occur when a group of men includes two members who have never met before. Since everybody else has greeted one another with a bold embrace, the unfamiliar pair are left with two options:

1) Acknowledge each other with the traditional handshake and risk appearing cold and out of step with the warmth exhibited by the rest of the group.

2) Briefly take hold of a man they have only just been introduced to and squeeze him tightly. If one is radically smaller than the other he will be forced to rest his head on the other man's chest like a child in need of comfort.

Either way it is vital both participants choose the same option. There are few things sadder than watching a chap bound forwards, arms outstretched, only for his target to recoil in horror.

It's crucial to read the warning signs appropriately before you lean in for the hug: arms clasped tightly to the side of his body and a look of terror are giveaways. Rapidly but smoothly, readjust your lunge and proffer a hand instead.

As a compromise you can accompany the shake with a gentle slap on the back. Because nothing says, 'Hey, you seem like a great guy who I'd like to get to know' better than a slap.

Bets

If you want a man to humiliate himself, simply bet that he can't. Only the most enlightened fellow can resist a challenge to his capabilities, even if it's his ability to eat a chicken vindaloo while swimming across a dangerous stretch of water, wearing his late grandmother's favourite ballgown.

Bivouac building

On the whole, most men are confident they would be just fine if they somehow found themselves marooned deep behind enemy lines and in need of improvised shelter. This confidence is based on nothing more than a mistaken belief in an innate survivalist instinct and the fact that they've watched Bear Grylls a couple of times on TV.

Anyone who has been on a father-child bonding expedition, or witnessed one from a safe distance, will have noticed that shelter-building activities are quickly monopolised by the adult males while their offspring run around looking for things to burn, or sit mournfully sharpening sticks and wondering what their Xboxes are up to while they're away.

You should think twice about forcing your child to spend a night in a self-built bivouac – it's likely to be the first time he realises you aren't good at everything. There's no going back after that.

How to build a bivouac

Step 1: Start to build your shelter well before nightfall. Find two sturdy sticks of equal length, ideally around 5ft long, both of which split into forks at one end.

Step 2: If you have a knife, sharpen the non-forked end of each stick into a point. Drive the pointed ends into the ground about 4ft apart.

Step 3: Take a third straight branch and place it horizontally across the forks of the supporting sticks. You have now built the frame.

Step 4: Now begin on the back wall. This should lean away from the prevailing wind, leaving the open side of your bivouac facing the campfire. Gather more branches and rest them against the horizontal support until you have created a screen.

Step 5: Weave smaller sticks, large leaves, ferns, reeds etc. through the screen to render your shelter waterproof. In tropical climes, banana plant and coconut tree leaves are particularly good.

Step 6: Place larger branches on top of your waterproof screen to prevent your bivouac blowing away in a light breeze.

Step 7: When your shelter proves less waterproof than hoped, make a mental note to book a B&B next year.

Bleeding radiators

Since the 1970s, when central heating became a common feature of modern living, men have spent around 67 per cent of their time at home wondering why it's so cold even though the thermostat is set to 28°C.

Those who know how to bleed radiators spend the other 33 per cent of their time gently pressing their palms against them to identify which ones are failing to provide heat in a uniform manner. They can then triumphantly announce to anyone within earshot that 'these radiators need bleeding'.

Bleeding radiators is a relatively simple task: all you need is a radiator key and a son-in-law to raise your eyebrows at and fix with a 'is there a reason you can't do this?' stare. The great value in understanding how to bleed a radiator is that, although it is no more taxing than most other everyday tasks, the hiss of trapped air being released and the gurgle of approaching water suggest you are bravely holding back plumbing Armageddon with your technical knowhow.

Bungee jumping

Blokes who bungee jump are allergic to simple pleasures such as having a cup of tea and doing the crossword. They are a nightmare to go on holiday with.

(See also: Base jumping, page 21)

'The greatest deception men suffer is from their own opinions.'

Leonardo da Vinci

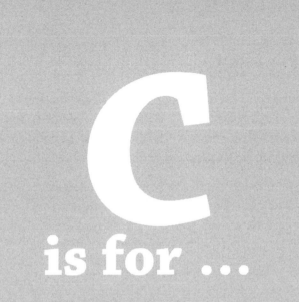

C

is for ...

Catching spiders

When a loved one screams, it is a man's natural instinct to remain seated and keep watching the telly. However, nine times out of ten his sense of duty will override this urge and he will leap into action.

When he reaches the bathroom to find a spider cowering by a plughole his response will be: 'Don't worry, it's far more scared of you than you are of it.' He won't mention that he is absolutely petrified.

He will then catch the spider and release it safely outside where, confused by its unusual surroundings, it will wander around in vain looking for a skirting board to sleep behind before being eaten by a hedgehog. However, its rescuer will believe he has added to his reputation within the household as a fearless yet humane individual who would have made a fine campaigner against poverty and injustice had accountancy not proved such a temptation.

How to catch a spider

Step 1: Remain calm, British spiders do not kill. If you're unlucky enough to find one that does, at least you'll die knowing you've discovered a new species.

Step 2: Assess the size of the spider and find a transparent container large enough to catch it in. Remember a spider will always outwit an ill-equipped man.

Step 3: Find a stiff piece of card that is bigger than the container to slip beneath it.

Step 4: Wait for the spider to settle on a flat surface.

Step 5: Approach slowly, gently placing the container over it. If you rush this part of the process you may accidentally amputate one of the spider's legs.

Step 6: Slide the card under the container.

Step 7: If you are not on the ground floor, do not throw it out of the nearest window. Spiders do not fly.

Step 8: Calmly walk the container downstairs and out the backdoor until you arrive at the nearest bush. Deposit the spider.

Step 9: Quickly go back inside. Check that it hasn't followed you or hidden in your turn-ups.

Channel-hopping

Give a man a TV remote and a digital TV and he'll keep himself amused for hours. Men live in constant fear that something better is happening somewhere else. Even though nothing better is ever happening on ITV4. Life is too short to bother reading the programme guide when you can hop through hundreds of channels every thirty minutes, steadfastly ignoring the mounting evidence that a man's short cut is always the longest way around.

Chanting

Chanting is the socially acceptable face of singing. A man cannot belt out his favourite show tune in public without expecting ridicule from his friends; he can, however, begin a tuneless chant about a football team and be fairly sure others will join in. This kind of male group singing is a bonding and cathartic experience. It is also often the precursor to violence.

Chat-up lines

Men fall back on chat-up lines in the hope that a well-rehearsed bon mot will enable them to bypass the conversational legwork usually associated with winning a girl's phone number, especially if the pub shuts in five minutes. But lines such as: 'I was told at school to follow my dreams, so I'm going to follow you home', and: 'If I said you had a beautiful body, would you hold it against me?', aren't always as successful as a man might hope.

Cheek-kissing clumsiness

The surest of men are shot through with doubt when cheek kissing erupts around them. It raises many troubling questions, including: how do women know with such instinctive ease when they are in a single-kiss situation and should not, under any circumstances, go looking for a second? How do they avoid tilting their heads in such a way it appears a snog is in the offing? And where the hell was I when this was taught at school?

Once a man finally thinks he has it sorted you can throw him back into a world of chaos, disorder and confusion by whispering in his ear: 'Did you know, in Belgium they kiss three times?'

(See also: Bear hugs, page 22)

Collecting and sharpening sticks

Leave a man in a wood with a knife and it will take him precisely thirty-four seconds to find a stick and absentmindedly begin sharpening it. Even though he's got a ready-made moussaka in the fridge at home, his primeval subconscious is preparing him to skewer a squirrel for dinner.

Conspiracy theories

There is no one so fervent as a conspiracy theorist. Men are particularly susceptible to conspiracy theories because they enjoy the sense of superiority that comes with knowing more than anyone else and often find real-world complexities just a little too complex to cope with.

You can identify a conspiracy theorist by dropping into conversation statements like: 'If Princess Diana can die in a terrible road accident we all can.' He will look at you scornfully and reply: 'Or maybe Prince Philip planned Diana's death to stop her revealing he is, in fact, king of the platypuses. A secretive species that, as well as being one of only two mammals to lay eggs, runs the world's financial system.'

He may also offer to take you to see all the supporting evidence he has been gathering, which will be plastered across the walls of his home-made bomb shelter.

Cycling

Ever since Britain added cycling to the list of sitting-down sports it excels at, millions of middle-aged men have taken to packaging their bodies in exuberant Lycra™ and pedalling around inappropriately narrow country lanes. Indeed the popularity of the sport has earned the acronym MAMIL, middle-aged man in Lycra™, an entry in some dictionaries.

The most committed MAMIL seeks to improve his performance by shaving his legs, simultaneously reducing air resistance and realising the widespread male desire to possess the gleaming hairless calf muscles of a catwalk model. You can spot his smooth pins in artful Instagram shots uploaded to Facebook after cycling club trips to the Pyrenees. And when you're in a queue of traffic waiting impatiently to pass him as he labours up a hill.

Cycling has much to offer a man embarking on a midlife crisis. It is an opportunity to prove he is still a physically capable individual within a supportive peloton of like-minded people. It also provides an excuse to lavish thousands of pounds on hand-made carbon fibre bikes and accessories – such as meters that measure the wattage of power a rider generates – that aren't absolutely necessary for a fortysomething amateur. Not to mention the fact that hanging about the house in a pair of revealing padded shorts is a great way to encourage teenage children to go out for some fresh air.

Importantly, cycling avoids the downsides associated with the more traditional interests of bored middle-aged men: affairs with younger women (notoriously bad for a marriage); sports cars (ineffective in the fight against a burgeoning body mass index); marathon running (limited scope for expensive technology) and alcoholism (all of the above).

(See also: Obstacle course fanaticism, page 134)

D

is for ...

Deconstructing TV shows

'I was fascinated by the way *Breaking Bad* placed an anti-heroic narrative arc, laced with tragic Shakespearean overtones, within the contemporary debate about public health subsidies and narcotics policy.' Because men can't help but take the fun out of your favourite TV shows.

Deodorising to excess

No man wants to be THAT man: the one responsible for the whiff of body odour that hangs almost imperceptibly, but unmistakably, in many of the nation's offices and across its entire public transport system.

In a bid to avoid olfactory shame men can often be found coating much of their upper bodies with sweat-busting chemicals. An enthusiastic deodoriser will spray an arc from his elbow to a point just below the ribcage, lingering for an extra few seconds as he passes the underarm. This should always be done in a ventilated setting, ideally an open field, and is the reason you

may feel slightly light-headed when entering a male changing room.

If using a roll-on he will work from the centre of his armpit in a spiral motion until he is at its outer reaches, occasionally skirting the chest area before retreating.

However, no matter how much deodorant a man applies, the key to maintaining a pleasant odour is a regime of regular cleansing. A fact the average teenage boy has yet to grasp.

Discussing roads

When a man asks a recently arrived male guest if he has had a good journey, he isn't really interested in his wellbeing, he is hoping to initiate a conversation that will allow him to tell the tired traveller about a little-known B-road that would have saved him half an hour.

Luckily, after five hours on the M6, the recently arrived man is happy to indulge in a road discussion because he is too drained to talk about anything more complicated. Of course, the only place he really wants to be at that moment is where he's just come from: home.

Any children present will listen in awe to their fathers, mesmerised by a strange tongue that involves an incomprehensible jumble of M1s, A3s and B592s off A66s. Little do they know one day when they grow up they'll suddenly find they too are fluent in roadspeak.

'The less men think, the more they talk.'

Charles de Montesquieu

Drinking games

Drinking games rely on a dangerous combination of two of man's greatest weaknesses: pride and alcohol. Few actually enjoy the experience but a young, impressionable man will feel compelled to join in when asked, because turning down the opportunity to become so inebriated he wets the bed for the first time since infant school would bring shame upon him.

Once one person has agreed to the game a domino effect takes hold, with each man who topples placing even more pressure on the next to join the fray. This is most prevalent during Freshers' Week in university towns, because new students will sign up to anything. Including juggling clubs.

Apart from the danger of hospitalisation, the problem with drinking games is there is never a clear result, which brings into question its right to be called a game. The more one person is forced to drink, the more likely he is to lose and be forced to drink more. But if everybody else involved is paying to get him drunk, who is the real loser?

E
is for …

Embellishing sporting achievements

At least 80 per cent of the male population either had a trial with a professional football team or were picked for the county rugby squad. The other 20 per cent were the lead in the school play and were '*this* close' to being recruited by a top London agent after a particularly moving drama department production of *Evita*.

These are not outright lies but, rather, the innocent misrememberings of men who in reality wrote a letter to Manchester United when they were ten and never heard back. Men like to think they are authors of their own destiny who only failed to make it in their chosen sport because of their decision to take up smoking and going to the pub.

Once they become fathers they can regularly be found on playing fields shouting at their sons who bloody well could play for England if only they tried a little harder.

Evading difficult emotional conversations

Ask a man how he is feeling and he will invariably reply 'not bad'. Tell him you need to talk and he will start looking around for escape routes.

Emotional conversations are often the prelude to change. Once a relationship has been established, men quickly fall into a regular pattern of daily rituals (see Relationship laziness, page 162); they are comfortable in this and don't envisage altering it too much until they retire, when they'll simply replace the work part of the day with bridge classes and trips to the M&S cafe.

However, when a man's partner says: 'I'm leaving unless you stop taking me for granted and start making an effort', it's a sign he should think about tweaking his habits a little before he reaches pensionable age. Unfortunately, for creatures of habit this is a troubling prospect.

Extreme eating

Being a human being has so many downsides: we are conscious that we are eventually going to die and before we do we will probably have to do Powerpoint presentations using words and phrases such as 'learnings' and 'consumer insight'. Worst of all, we can't curl up and take a nap in the boiler cupboard whenever we like. However, making up for all of this is the daily joy we derive from food.

Unlike other species, we eat for pleasure, not merely to survive. And when humanity is on to a good thing it is in man's nature to take that good thing too far and ruin it, possibly killing himself in the process.

Extreme eating is most common in societies in which men believe they have mastered the art of surviving and thriving. Pointless acts of food-based bravado, such as munching on a kilo of Trinidad Scorpion chillies or eating a 3ft-wide burger in under an hour, are a challenge to nature; and nature is normally happy to rise to that challenge in the form of a heart attack.

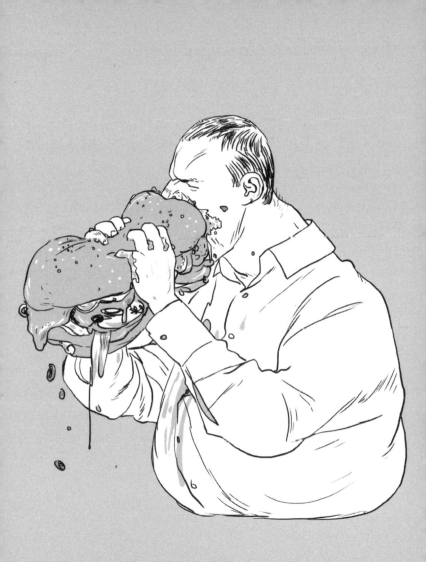

F

is for ...

Fantasy football

To those who don't take part in fantasy football leagues, constructing an imaginary team, trading players with imaginary money and triumphing over equally imaginary opponents seems like an odd, if not worryingly delusional, pursuit.

The committed football fantasist spends approximately 98 per cent of his working Friday considering which players to transfer into his side before the Saturday morning deadline. To the non-fantasist such potentially career-crippling commitment to an online game adds a pointless level of danger to an already worthless pastime.

However, managing a fantasy football team is not completely without merit. Here are three ways it can help in life:

1) The football fantasist becomes adept at sensing his boss's presence and speedily minimising offending windows on his desktop.

2) At his next job interview – if he hasn't mastered the above this could come along very soon – he can justifiably claim to have experienced managing a £50 million budget.

3) When he takes charge of his eight-year-old's Sunday League team he'll be able to implement the 4-2-3-1 formation and high-tempo pressing game that he has been perfecting in his imaginary world.

Fear of commitment

Men like to think they are spontaneous beings even though their social lives generally revolve around the same four friends, the same two pubs and a monthly poker night. When the time comes to move in with somebody, enter a lifelong union or, worst of all, have a baby, they fear they will be transformed from freewheeling adventurers into housebound lapdogs. To be fair, having a baby does just this.

Of course, as soon as they do commit to another person, their lives immediately become more interesting. Their partners take them to pubs they haven't been to before, introduce them to exciting new people and plan trips to exotic places they've never heard of, thus reducing the time available to go for a pint down the road. Which is exactly what they feared would happen.

Fear of holding newborn babies

Despite the fact that men take an immense amount of pride in being able to throw and catch a ball competently, deep down they fear their hands are actually accident-prone lumps of skin and bone that could betray them at any moment. When presented with a baby that is not their own, this is the thought that overwhelms them – no man wants to leave a new mother with the impression he couldn't be trusted on a cricket field.

Conversely, they are wildly overconfident with their own newborns, holding them nonchalantly over a hot stove with one hand while draining pasta with the other, freed by the knowledge that their partners already know they're rubbish at cricket.

'There are only two forces that unite men – fear and interest.'

Napoleon Bonaparte

How to hold a newborn baby

Step 1: Bear in mind that, although they are more robust than they appear, you should never drop a newborn baby.

Step 2: Lift him by sliding one hand under his bottom and one under his head, resting his back on your forearm. Alternatively, put your hands under his shoulders and hold his head with your fingers.

Step 3: Once lifted, cradle him in the crook of your elbow or hold him upright against your chest. Remember to support his head at all times during this process – failure to do so will lead to disconcerting wobbling.

Step 4: Once you are holding him avoid sudden movements – he is used to the tranquillity of the womb. You must attempt to replicate this with your arms.

Step 5: If he starts nuzzling at your nipple area and opening his mouth it means he is hungry. Hand him back immediately; you cannot help here.

Fighting in pubs

Every Friday night in a pub near you men will butt heads and growl rhetorical questions such as: 'You want some, do ya?' at each other, as concerned girlfriends scream: 'He's not worth it, babes!' in the background.

Most of these men are perfectly reasonable humans in their day-to-day lives: good citizens who hold doors open for others, forward cute kitten gifs to their friends and refrain from threatening face-splitting violence if somebody spills their drink or accidentally glances in their general direction. But in the macho environment of the pub even the slightest of slights must be aggressively addressed.

Fortunately these stand-offs rarely develop into full-blown bar fights. The majority of men have never punched anyone before, especially not in the head area, and suspect it might not be as much fun as it looks in films.

Fire lighting

Men are irresistibly drawn to the act of lighting a fire. Fire is the ultimate multi-purpose all-natural gadget: it generates heat, cooks food, is a source of light and keeps dangerous animals at a safe distance. It also provides the perfect excuse to construct a little house out of sticks before burning it to the ground, satisfying man's contrasting urges to build and destroy.

Most importantly, a fire provides a focal point for a group of men who have nothing in common apart from the fact that they've all been forced to go on the same friends-and-family camping weekend.

Nearly all men claim to be capable of coaxing a flame into life using nothing but flint and tinder or by rubbing two sticks together. This will put them several steps ahead of those who do not possess such skills when the world is plunged into a nuclear winter and someone drops the last box of matches in a radioactive puddle.

(See also: Bivouac-building, page 25)

How to light a fire without matches

Step 1: Gather some tinder. The bark shavings of birch and cedar trees are particularly combustible. Or, if you have a coconut to hand, the fine fibres of its husk are ideal.

Step 2: Make sure your tinder isn't wet. If you can, bring some you've been drying at home; only those who haven't thought to do so regard this as cheating.

Step 3: Remove the bark from a dry tree branch – willow, cedar and juniper are all good varieties to use – and use a knife or sharp stone to plane down the branch to create a flat surface on one side. Cut a groove about 8in long into the flat surface.

Step 4: Push the sharpened end of a thin stick from the same tree back and forth along the groove at a 45° angle until small embers appear. This is tedious work – if possible get a child to do it for you.

Step 5: Tip the embers into your tinder bundle and *gently* blow into it. Gently is the operative word here – blow too hard and you will either extinguish your fire before it's even started or shower your face in sparks.

Step 6: Once the tinder is lit, place it inside a miniature tepee made of sticks and kindling.

Step 7: Continue blowing lightly until your fire is burning strongly.

Flexing muscles in the mirror

When a man passes a mirror in the privacy of his own home it is an automatic invitation to curl a bicep or tighten an abdominal muscle. There are two prominent types of muscle-flexing male:

1) The soft-tissue obsessive who has foregone bog-standard relations with other human beings to enter into a committed relationship with a pair of dumb-bells. He is keen to ensure his body ripples in all the relevant places and will impress passers-by when he is on his way to the gym or shopping for protein shakes.

2) The mostly sedentary male between the ages of twenty-five and forty. He still engages in some exercise but is drifting inexorably towards a life that revolves almost entirely around sitting down. When he finds himself in front of a mirror with his top off he tenses in a bid to reassure himself that the hint of definition that briefly appears proves he is still the toned sprite of yesteryear.

How to do a press-up

Step 1: Find a space that can accommodate your prone body and where it is unlikely to become a hazard to passing pedestrians.

Step 2: Place your hands on the ground slightly wider than shoulder width apart.

Step 3: Rest the balls of your feet on the ground at a width that is comfortable and stable.

Step 4: Make sure your body forms a strong, diagonal line from your head to your heels. If your backside is above your head – or your stomach, even a large one, is touching the floor – readjust.

Step 5: Once you have formed the perfect press-up position lower yourself, keeping your body rigid, until your nose almost touches the ground.

Step 6: Resist the temptation to lie down at this point.

Step 7: Push yourself back up into the press-up position.

Step 8: If capable, repeat steps 5 to 7.

G

is for...

Golfing holidays

When men are young they go on holiday with three aims: to drink, to get a tan and to have lots of sex. Usually they achieve one-and-a-half of these goals: they get drunk and they get sunburnt.

When men are older and have families, they too spend their holidays drinking and burning. They also spend much of their time wishing their children would make some friends and sod off. This is why parents are the only people glad to get back to work after a holiday.

The golfing break stands halfway between these two holidays. Like the family holiday it is usually taken by males over thirty who have children; but, like the holidays of their carefree youths, they will actually enjoy it. Also like both, they will drink and burn.

Playing golf isn't the primary objective of a golfing holiday. The primary objective is to create a trip that neither their wives nor partners nor, most importantly, children will want to join them on. Obviously some wives and partners like playing golf, which is why some men also go on fishing holidays.

How to master basic golf etiquette

Step 1: Be aware that most clubs won't let you in if you are wearing jeans or trainers. The golfing weekend capsule wardrobe should include: blazer, smart-casual slacks, monogrammed polo shirts or short-sleeved summer shirts, peaked sports cap or visor, v-neck sweaters (pastel shades optional). Garish colours are also de rigueur – think Alan Partridge meets a smart-casual children's entertainer.

Step 2: If you are taking a woman, to avoid an awkward situation later on, check she will be allowed into the bar.

Step 3: Remain silent when one of your party, or anybody on a nearby hole, is playing a shot. Do not clench your fist and whisper 'yes' when their ball finds a water hazard.

Step 4: Replace any divots you create on the fairway, but not on the tee.

Step 5: After use, leave bunkers how you would wish to find them by tidying up with the rake provided. When you have finished place the rake to the side of the bunker.

Step 6: If you are spending a lot of time looking for lost balls, ask any groups following yours if they would like to play through. It is important to understand the meaning of obscure expressions such as 'playing through'. This will make you sound as if you know what you are talking about.

Step 7: When you finally get there, do not lay your golf bag on the green.

Step 8: Repair damage caused by your shoes on the green only after everybody has finished the hole.

Step 9: Always put your blazer on before entering the clubhouse to reduce the chances of offending the members.

'Golf appeals to the idiot in us and the child. Just how childlike golf players become is proven by their frequent inability to count past five.'

John Updike

Gaming in large groups

Gathering together to take part in an evening devoted to the annihilation of a virtual enemy is popular among groups of young, usually single, men. Friendships are welded through the medium of communal video-game violence and the act of passing bowls of tangy cheese tortilla chips around a room. It is one of the few occasions when men will work harmoniously together towards a mutually beneficial goal, which, on this occasion, is to kill, kill, KILL!

Although online gaming is also popular it doesn't offer the same socially uplifting experience. Once a gamer has successfully blown the face off an extra-terrestrial with the help of a teenager in Uzbekistan, he is left alone in a dark room with nothing to show for it but a thumbs-up emoticon. On the plus side he has just demonstrated that in the event of an alien invasion it may well be possible to organise a cross-border resistance movement.

Growing facial hair

Facial hair requires urgent state regulation, but is one area of modern male life in which successive governments have refused to intervene. Men simply can't be trusted to grow it properly on their own. These beards are of particular concern:

1) **The teen beard:** wispy, patchy and grown for the sole purpose of fooling a bouncer into thinking its owner isn't underage, it is the closest a man will ever come to cultivating actual cotton wool on his face.

2) **The incomplete beard:** a beard without a moustache, or which doesn't meet at the chin, is like a song without a chorus, or a jigsaw puzzle without the corners.

3) **The overly shaped beard:** designed to prove the wearer is a sharp operator, this beard is undermined by the fact it looks as if he has drawn it on using a felt-tip and a set square.

4) **The goatee:** does it confer gravitas or remind onlookers of a toddler who has just stuffed his face with chocolate ice cream?

1)

2)

3)

4)

5)

6)

5) **The unkempt full beard:** adopted by many because of its counter-cultural roots, this beard has become so popular with hipsters you are now twenty-eight times more likely to get a job in digital media if you have a shambolic fuzz of facial hair obscuring your mouth.

6) **The soul patch:** a tuft of hair that sits in the dent below a man's mouth on an otherwise smooth face, it suggests the owner once had a terrible shaving accident involving his bottom lip and is now too afraid to go near it with a razor.

'Men are the sport of circumstances, when the circumstances seem the sport of men.'

Lord Byron

Gruelling family holidays

Every now and then a father will decide he should try to instil an inquiring spirit and a get-up-and-go sense of adventure in his children by cancelling the family holiday to Spain and booking a hiking expedition in the Lake District that incorporates day trips to the Wordsworth Museum and Museum of Lakeland Life and Industry. This is despite the fact that everybody in the family, including him, would much rather spend two weeks lounging by a pool or, if it's not too much of a walk, on a beach.

It is a mistake he is only likely to make once: it will rain relentlessly, his youngest will have blisters the size of Cumbria by day three and his eldest will be too busy texting his friends and contemplating divorcing his parents to appreciate the views when the cloud finally lifts. Of course, there are children out there who enjoy engaging in cultural pursuits with their mums and dads. But they're always somebody else's.

Grumpiness

Among adult males there are two predominant mental ages: pubescent and old-age pensioner. Half haven't progressed beyond the maturity of a fourteen-year-old, the rest pulled on a pair of slippers and lit a metaphorical pipe in their mid-twenties and haven't stopped grumbling since.

'Whenever ideas fail, men invent words.'

Martin H. Fischer

H
is for ...

Haggling

There are those who haggle and those who find negotiating the equivalent of a 20p reduction on a poncho tedious, tight-fisted and humiliating. The former are most often men.

Hagglers often emerge during backpacking trips and establish themselves on holidays that follow, eventually reaching the point at which any transaction conducted in a foreign language is up for debate. By the time they hit middle age they are accompanied by permanently embarrassed children.

Strangely, the more expensive an item is, and the more opulent the environment in which it is sold, the less likely a man is to haggle. This is because haggling isn't about saving money, it's about walking away from a commercial exchange with the sense that you have won. And in very expensive shops it is the person who can afford to pay the most who is deemed to have succeeded in life.

Hair gel

Gel is the super glue of the hair-styling world, a product so powerful it can transform thousands of strands of hair into a solid, immovable, glistening object. Unlike its more subtle siblings – wax, mousse and spray – hair gel is used by men who feel the need to make a bold statement with their coiffure. This is known as Cristiano Ronaldo Syndrome.

The young male geller is attempting to tell his friends and family he has discovered hair products and isn't afraid to use them, especially if it's the night of the school disco. It is a rite of passage nearly all men go through. The older male hair-geller is indicating to the world that he is ambitious and in control of his life. Nothing will stand in his way, certainly not his slick-backed concrete mop, which isn't going anywhere anytime soon. He might be an estate agent. In both cases they have yet to learn less is more.

High-fiving

If you are ever left wondering whether it is appropriate to perform a high five, remember this rule: it is never appropriate to perform a high five unless you are American. The successful high five requires two people brimming with unabashed enthusiasm and completely lacking in cynicism. It is highly unlikely you'll ever find two men of this persuasion in the same place at the same time if you live in Britain, unless you work in sales.

The habitual high fiver is merely attempting to draw attention to the fact that he has done something great. This offends some of the finest British traditions, including:

1) A distaste for self-congratulatory actions. When we succeed we should be humble to the point of denying whatever success we've just experienced was anything other than a complete mistake that has ruined our lives.

2) Resentment of other people's success. Why celebrate somebody else's promotion when the only reason he has achieved it is because you've been cruelly overlooked by management time and time again?

Hidden fondness for soap operas

Dads in particular are guilty of striding into a front room, glaring at the TV and shouting, 'What's this rubbish?', before sitting down and interrupting everybody's enjoyment with a stream of questions: 'She's done *what* with Steve McDonald?!', 'Max Branning is sleeping with *who*?', 'Will they ever install traffic calming measures in Albert Square? How many people have to die?'

Men like to think they are above light entertainment but that doesn't stop them catching up on *Hollyoaks* when everybody else is out of the house.

Hiding in sheds

When a man is in his shed he hopes his nearest and dearest will assume he is up to something useful. It is, after all, where he keeps many of his tools. However, he is more likely to be indulging in a slightly embarrassing hobby – the painting of model trains, planes or soldiers, perhaps – or simply sitting on a well-worn chair and working his way through the Screwfix catalogue.

He knows he won't be disturbed because nobody else is silly enough to want to while away their spare time in a space that is home to a colony of woodlice and a ferocious draught.

'Buy a man a beer and he wastes an hour. Teach a man to brew and he wastes a lifetime.'

Charles Papazian

Home brewing

Making your own beer used to be the preserve of middle-aged men with soft spots for early morning Open University TV programmes and beards that could house entire ecosystems. The beards are still there, but today they are on the faces of younger, trendier men who prune them into pointy shapes for no good reason.

Ale has been rebranded as 'craft beer' by sexy independent breweries that aren't in it for the money but charge £4 a bottle, and exported from working men's clubs to Shoreditch pubs where everybody dresses so ironically it's impossible to tell who is genuinely wearing clothes.

These new drinkers have swelled the home-brewing ranks, eager to create their very own barrel of Ocelot's Beef Jacket or Badger's Arse Smirk in their garage.

How to home brew

Step 1: Buy a home brewing starter kit. This will provide you with all the equipment and ingredients you need.

Step 2: Always clean the kit to avoid impurities distorting the flavour of your first brew.

Step 3: Empty the malt into the brewing bucket, add water and stir.

Step 4: Mix yeast into the liquid before covering and setting aside in a warm place for one to two weeks.

Step 5: As your brew ferments it will bubble. When the bubbling stops it is time to move on to the next stage.

Stage 6: Check it is definitely time to move on to the next stage by measuring the density of the mixture using the hydrometer provided; the reading you are looking for will vary depending on the type of beer you are brewing.

Stage 7: Add priming sugars to the batch to help it carbonate, then transfer your beer to a barrel or into bottles. Leave in a warm place for three days.

Stage 8: Move to a cold environment to allow the sediment to settle. This could take up to four weeks – you will be tempted to taste your beer during this time. Don't. It is important that it is not disturbed.

Stage 9: Now you can drink the beer. If it is your first attempt at home brewing do not be disheartened if it tastes horrific.

I
is for ...

Ignoring instruction manuals

Why sit down and read an instruction manual when it's possible to construct a flat-pack multi-unit storage cabinet entirely by instinct? Step-by-step guides are for the benefit of slow-witted souls who do not possess the practical acumen to transform a pile of MDF into a simple piece of Nordic furniture – referring to them is a sign of failure. Of course, some people believe ten minutes spent reading a small booklet is a clever investment considering it will save several hours swearing at a hinge later on. But what do they know?

If figures were available for such things they would no doubt show that most domestic products that break or fall apart at a cruelly young age were built, programmed or maintained by a man who didn't read the instructions.

Inability to admit mistakes

Men do not make mistakes. They are compelled into actions they would otherwise not have taken by forces beyond their control. Anything that breaks in a man's hands has a 'flawed design' and 'if you didn't want me to drill through the shaver-socket wiring you shouldn't have asked for a mirror in the bathroom'.

The place where men make the least mistakes is in the car. They are never wrong when it comes to directions, are always on the right side of a road-rage incident (see page 164) and only struggle to get into a space because everybody else has parked so badly.

Inaccurate peeing

With a little time and effort adult men, like dogs, can be domesticated. Once they start cohabiting most learn not to wee on their own toilet seat.

However, when a man is freed from the oppressive bathroom hygiene regime he endures at home he loses all sense of toilet decorum. This manifests itself in several ways:

1) He leaves the toilet seat down while urinating, an act of rebellion against polite society far worse than leaving it up after his visit that has the effect of giving him a smaller target to hit. This initiates a vicious urinary circle since the more pee that lands on the seat, the less likely the next man is to lift it up.

2) He experiments with a no-hands approach to urinating, dangerously leaving his thrust-forward hips in charge.

3) He loses focus and starts absent-mindedly perusing the bathroom wall art. In a family home this will consist of the lesser accomplishments of any children living there – piano grades one to four – and jaunty limericks asking you not to flush tampons down the

loo. In a pub it will be artfully naked women, vintage gig posters or prostate cancer warnings. At some point he will look down to see he has spent thirty seconds peeing on the wall, his leg or, worse, the leg of a man standing next to him.

4) He takes a couple of steps back and tests whether he has the ability to hit the water from 3ft with a perfect arc. If he is outside he will try and pee as high as he can up a wall or tree.

Inevitably alcohol exacerbates the situation, which is why sitting down on a male pub toilet seat is the equivalent of asking every bloke at the bar to pee on your bum.

Inappropriate jokes

Fraught, emotionally charged situations are rarely where a man feels most comfortable. Luckily he has a back catalogue of cracking jokes to lighten the mood and reduce the chances he'll have to take part in any difficult conversations that might involve crying. For example:

1) Don't worry, there are plenty of fish in the sea and some of them have sensible haircuts and good job prospects.

2) It could be worse: imagine if our flight was delayed for two days and we didn't have this comfy marble-effect airport floor to sleep on!

3) Honestly, it looks perfectly natural. Did they use the spray tan gun or the spray tan machine gun?

Inflexible thermostat setting

Although they are designed to be adjusted, a man believes you should never go back to a set thermostat, let alone turn one up.

Unfortunately, everybody he lives with would rather use a little more gas than wear a winter coat in bed. The resulting tit-for-tat cycle of thermostat adjustments is one that afflicts households throughout the land. Man reasons that increasing the temperature to 28°C will create a furnace, and excessively lowers the thermostat in response, thus ensuring everybody will soon be too cold again. That's no way to live.

What he craves is consistency – there really is no need to heat any living space above 20°C and therefore no need to touch the thermostat. Although he may sell this as a stand against the environmentally destructive impact of fossil fuel, he's really trying to save money.

How to use your central heating efficiently

Step 1: If your boiler is older than you, buy a new one. This is a costly exercise but will pay off in the long term as long as you are not planning to move house in the near future.

Step 2: Turn your thermostat down. The higher it is set has no impact on how quickly a room heats up.

Step 3: To find the optimum temperature for your home set the thermostat to 18°C and turn it up 1°C each day until you hit upon an internal climate the whole family can agree on.

Step 4: If possible introduce separate heating circuits and thermostats to each zone of your house and turn them down in those you use less often.

Step 5: If you have both a room thermostat and thermostatic radiator valves (TRVs), set the TRVs slightly higher than the thermostat. If you do not have a room thermostat apply Step 3 to the TRVs.

Step 6: Do not leave your boiler's electronic programmer on its default setting. Adjust it to reflect your use of the home and prevent unnecessary heating. Electronic programmers should only be approached when you have plenty of time to read the instructions and are in a calm state of mind.

Step 7: Make sure radiators can circulate heat effectively by removing covers, nearby furniture and drying underwear.

Step 8: Replace all radiators now in use with expensive vintage-effect versions.

Interest in military history

Bump into the man-on-the-street these days and he is unlikely to have seen action in a theatre of war, unlike, say, in the 1920s or 1950s when a good proportion of adult males had witnessed someone's head being blown off in a recent global conflict. Which makes it strange that these periods are often romanticised as more innocent times.

There is a small part of the modern male psyche that finds this a cause for regret, because this part of the male psyche thinks world wars are great.

Normal rules do not apply during a world war. Suddenly graduates aren't scrambling to apply for jobs in multi-national corporations that will, within five years, fill them with self-loathing; they're scrambling across battlefields as part of a grand, history-defining narrative. And everybody has sex because they could be dead tomorrow, which isn't much of a compliment – 'Hey, let's just do it! The likelihood is you'll be mangled by a machine gun in the not-too-distant future so we won't have to have that awkward break-up chat' – but men will take it where they can get it.

If you leave out the bits that involve drowning in freezing North Atlantic waters, burning to death in a tank or being forced to search your own excrement for edible bits in a prisoner-of-war camp – and the fact everybody probably doesn't have loads of sex – world wars really are ace.

Fortunately, the closest most men will get to one is the History Channel.

'Nearly all men can stand adversity, but if you want to test a man's character, give him power.'

Abraham Lincoln

J

is for ...

J Joining secret societies

Most secret societies fade away, fated to live on only in the minds of conspiracy theorists (see page 37); others evolve into places where men gather to engage in ceremonial acts before swapping business cards.

As well as the obvious benefits that come with possessing a handshake that can unlock metaphorical doors, men enjoy the air of mystery that belonging to a secret society brings. That's why they'll happily drop hints that they are part of a secret society to anybody who'll listen.

Juicing

There is a juicing machine waiting patiently to be ushered out of hibernation in exactly 55.3 per cent of the nation's homes. It was bought when its owner was training for a marathon or just after he'd been given a warning about his cholesterol level.

At first creating home-made fruit smoothies is a revelation, partly because they taste so nice but mainly because they give drinkers a disproportionate sense of wellbeing: 'I can really feel the effect of the 7,980 kebabs I've eaten during my lifetime being washed away by the juice of fifteen kiwi fruits. I'm going to live forever!'

Gradually, however, peeling and slicing a dozen mangoes each week loses its allure, especially once a cloud of fruit flies has settled on every available surface in your kitchen. One day, as he cleans decomposing fruit from the hard-to-reach underside of his juicer blade, the previously enthusiastic smoothie maker will subconsciously decide to buy his next one from the organic cafe down the road. So begins the juicing machine's rapid decline into obsolescence.

Juggling

Not every man wants to perform in a circus – or develop
a career as a clown – but they would all like to be
able to juggle. Why? Because it is a simple skill that
is disproportionately impressive to those who have
yet to master it, usually young children. Once a man
can juggle, every decently filled fruit bowl he passes
suddenly becomes an opportunity to show off. And if
there's one thing all men want it is more opportunities
to show off.

How to juggle three balls

Step 1: Select the objects you wish to juggle. Clubs,
knives or anything that is on fire should be avoided
until you are more advanced. Palm-sized bean bags or
balls are ideal for beginners.

Step 2: Clear all breakable items from the area in which
you plan to juggle.

Step 3: Practise throwing one ball from hand to hand; it
should describe a consistent arc that peaks at eye level.

Step 4: Introduce a second ball. When the first ball reaches the top of its arc, throw the second ball at a slightly different trajectory with your other hand. Repeat and develop a throw-throw-catch-catch rhythm.

Step 5: Introduce a third ball. Holding two balls in your right hand (or vice versa if you are left-handed), begin by throwing one of them; when it reaches its peak throw the single ball in your left hand. As the second ball reaches its peak, catch the first ball in your left hand and throw the third ball with your right hand.

Step 6: Continue and perfect before moving on to the eggs.

'Boys will be boys, and so will a lot of middle-aged men.'

Kin Hubbard

K

is for ...

Karate kicking imaginary foes

Considering the combined cultural might of Hong Kong Phooey, Mr Miyagi and the Teenage Mutant Ninja Turtles, it's no surprise boys grow up with such reverence for the martial artist. This reverence doesn't wilt when the boy becomes a man, it merely graduates to a liking for Bruce Lee and a strongly held conviction that, when attacked, he could take out a gang of muggers with some kind of spinning kick.

And there's nothing to stop a man practising for such an event in the privacy of his own home, which is why he can sometimes be found swinging his leg above table corners or small children and shouting: 'HI *YA*'. This often results in tendon damage.

Kitchen fascism

Men are latecomers to the kitchen – several thousand years late – but they're making up for their tardiness in the twenty-first century. Naturally, many are crossing the line between helpful enthusiasm and an overzealous pursuit of the perfect sous vide foie gras.

Sharing a kitchen with this breed of cook is a testing experience: they will not take kindly to your input, even if all you've done is stir their red wine reduction. However, when you are cooking they will stand in the corner and ask questions such as: 'Do you think it needs a touch of foraged sorrel?' and 'Shouldn't you hay-smoke the lamb?'

Preparing dinner becomes a tediously overblown chore that involves finding the only butcher in the area who supplies pork from a pig that has been reared as a vegan. It may also involve tramping across the local playing field trying to find a herb that hasn't been soiled by a dog. This is especially frustrating because these fields are nearly always next to a supermarket.

How to cook a simple but impressive meal

Step 1: Start with an easy dish you can prepare earlier in the day, such as potted shrimp.

Step 2: To cook this, melt butter in a pan, heat the shrimp in the butter and add a pinch of nutmeg and cayenne pepper. Season and place in ramekins, pour over the remaining butter and put in the fridge to set. Serve with thick brown bread.

Step 3: Fall back on a guaranteed crowd-pleaser for your main course. Nobody, for example, will turn their nose up at a steak. Apart, possibly, from a vegetarian.

Step 4: Instead of making a complicated sauce for the steak, create a range of flavoured butters which you can call on at any moment. To make, mix butter with crushed peppercorns or a herb or spice of your choice, wrap in cling film and store in the freezer.

Step 5: Accompany with a stack of thick-cut oven chips or oven-cooked French fries, unless you have a deep fat fryer and actually want to use it.

Step 6: Add a watercress side salad dressed in olive oil, a squeeze of lemon and seasoning.

Step 7: Keep a supply of frozen summer fruits or berries. Blend them with sugar and a splash of water and drizzle the resulting coulis over cheesecake or chocolate brownies to create a fine-dining dessert.

Knowing the answer to everything

There is no limit to how clever some men think they are. It is physically impossible for such a man to withhold an opinion on any subject – from the situation in Gaza to the best way to domesticate a giraffe and which cider to drink with lavender crème brûlée – no matter how little experience he has of it.

Some, particularly taxi drivers, don't let the lack of a question stop them providing an extensive and wildly misinformed answer. Such men are most likely to embark on a confident explanation of a subject they know nothing about when talking to a woman, who, obviously, knows even less than they do. This is where the term 'mansplaining' comes from.

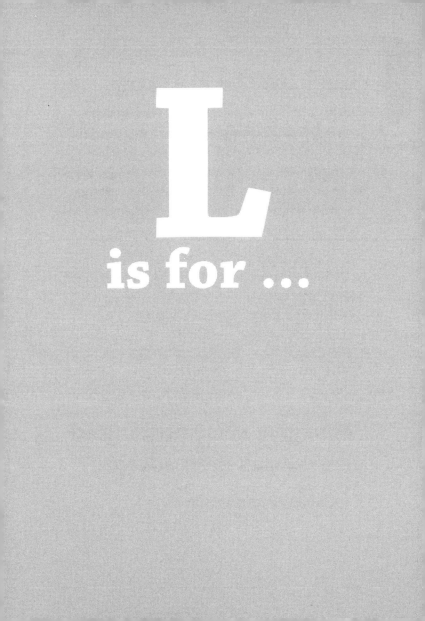

L

is for …

Lacklustre tidying

Tidying is not a job to be done well. It is a job to be done quickly. If putting away pots and pans involves rearranging the pots and pans cupboard, then the lacklustre tidier will simply find somewhere else to put them rather than go to all that trouble. This is why you can never find what you are looking for after a man has tidied up.

Equally, a tidy house is an invitation to sit down and start watching a box set. It is not an invitation to check the laundry basket for dirty washing or investigate whether the dishwasher needs emptying.

'Men give away nothing so liberally as their advice.'

François de La Rochefoucauld

Last-minute shopping

Even active and outwardly healthy males struggle to shop for more than an hour without exhibiting signs of chronic fatigue such as muscle pain, irritability and a desperate need to find out the football scores. That's why in most retail environments you'll find at least three men leaning against a wall and staring at a smartphone.

Men have an extremely low browsing tolerance and struggle to retain focus when presented with more than two different styles of jumper, let alone several shops selling several styles of jumper, not to mention cardigans. They prefer a clearly defined target and a pressing deadline, as if they are on a mission with the special forces – they get in and they get out, there's no time for messing around in enemy territory.

As when soldiers go off to combat, it is the friends and family at home who often suffer the most, in this case in the form of ill-thought-out and rashly judged Christmas and birthday presents.

How to buy a gift for your girlfriend

Step 1: Buy a present that demonstrates you have thought, however briefly, about the person you are giving it to.

Step 2: Consider personalising jewellery or buying an experience you can do together – check whether she has ever wanted to skydive first.

Step 3: If you decide to buy lingerie choose a style you think she will be comfortable wearing. Not a style you would like to see her in if she suddenly took up stripping. Check her size before purchasing – if unsure always underestimate.

Step 4: Ask the shop to gift-wrap the present: you will not do a better job.

Step 5: Always keep the receipt.

Late-night inebriated singing

Few men are immune to the emotional tug of a rousing anthemic song, especially if it's played at two in the morning and they've drunk a bottle of tequila. In many of the nation's clubs these songs are saved for the end of the night, when men are fluctuating erratically between wanting a fight and wanting to hug everybody.

The anthemic song prompts the affected man to grasp his friends around the shoulders and form a moving line or circle of howling humanity that bumps its way annoyingly around the dance floor. As they shriek the chorus to 'The Final Countdown', showering their mates in 50 per cent proof spit, those within the circle briefly experience a transcendent brotherly moment, which quickly dissipates when the lights come on and they realise all those involved are covered in beer and struggling to stand up.

This singing may continue in breakaway groups during post-club visits to fried chicken shops, on night buses and in hedges that cushion falls on the walk home from the bus stop.

Late-night inebriated philosophical conversations

Following closely in the tuneless tracks of late-night inebriated singing comes late-night inebriated profundity. It is in the quiet moments after an evening spent in a drum 'n' bass club performing a rhythmic impersonation of a traffic policeman with poor motor control, that a man feels most equipped to answer complex philosophical and political questions. If he were to try and operate heavy machinery or drive a car at this moment he would, however, be arrested immediately.

'An intelligent man is sometimes forced to be drunk to spend time with his fools.'

Ernest Hemingway

Lavish stag dos

In more sensible times a man was happy to celebrate the end of his bachelor days with ten pints of best and a game of pub skittles, before being stripped naked and tied to some street furniture. These days he expects his friends to accompany him on a four-day bender in Ljubljana.

At some point during such stag dos, usually when the first hangover kicks in, a man who was only invited to make up the numbers will quietly wonder why he's spending a month's wages to get hammered on foreign soil when he could do it just as effectively at home. If he has had to fork out for a food processor from the wedding gift list, having been beaten to the oven gloves, toast racks and napkins, then the extravagant expense will be even more upsetting.

Of course, when it's his turn he'll instruct his best man to book a plane to Las Vegas.

Learning to play the guitar

If you are a boy of school age, it is of far greater social advantage to be able to labour your way through three chords on an electric guitar than it is to have reached grade eight on the oboe and have a recital at the Royal Festival Hall in the diary.

Being a guitarist, preferably one in a band, is much sexier than being an accomplished exponent of almost any other instrument. That sexiness is multiplied several times over if you also own a distortion pedal. However, most teenage rock 'n' roll dreams die in a tableau of underwashed long hair and poorly attended school hall gigs.

It is not unusual for middle-aged men to take up the guitar when they realise they haven't mastered a new skill since they left education that wasn't related to an Excel spreadsheet. They are also gripped with regret that they decided against learning the oboe when they had the chance.

How to bluff playing the guitar

Step 1: Tune your guitar using an electronic tuner that senses which string you are playing so that you can get away with not knowing.

Step 2: Choose three chords to learn. Many of the greatest songs consist of only three chords – Bob Dylan carved a handy career out them. G, C and D are popular.

Step 3: Learn them using guitar chord charts, a form of musical notation that doesn't require you to be able to read music, which saves a lot of time.

Step 4: On a chord chart the vertical lines represent the strings; the line furthest to the right is the 'high E' string on a six-string guitar. The horizontal lines divide up the fretboard, the first fret is at the top of the chart

FIRST FRET →

E STRING

Step 5: A dark circle indicates which fret a string should be held down on, the number inside the circle indicates which finger to use.

Step 6: If there is a cross above a string you do not play it when strumming the chord. A small empty circle means you play the string but do not hold it down.

Step 7: Practise moving smoothly between chords. This will prove painful until your fingertips develop an attractive coating of hard skin.

Step 8: Find a song that uses these three chords such as 'Amazing Grace'.

Listen to it and take note of the rhythm.

Step 9: Learn the first verse by strumming the relevant chords as you sing the lyrics:

G C G
Amazing Grace, how sweet the sound,

D
That saved a wretch like me.

G C G
I once was lost, but now I'm found,

G D G
Was blind, but now I see

List-making

As far as men are concerned, shopping should be done in a spur-of-the-moment frenzy. A list forces a man to buy things like fabric softener and toilet paper when he really wants to fill his trolley with massive boxes of cereal and half-price beer or, if he's in Waitrose, several tubs of their exquisite stuffed olive selection.

However, put him in a pub with a group of other men and suddenly he is a great supporter of the list. He might prefer free will in the supermarket but he can't be expected to sustain a conversation for an entire evening without a little structure. Even the quietest of men become animated when discussing the top five Scottish full-backs of the 1970s or, in pubs that serve craft ale and bowls of salted cashew nuts, the top five post punk-era electro innovators.

M
is for ...

Making up nicknames

Parents go to an awful lot of trouble choosing what to call their children, so it's a shame a boy's name becomes redundant as soon as he enters secondary school. Here it is immediately deconstructed into something that is easier to blurt across a field while simultaneously chewing gum, smoking and snogging.

Once a nickname has taken hold among a group of friends it is impossible to shake off and will follow its owner to the grave. That's why when a man bumps into an old classmate who, rumour had it, got an erection during his GCSE Biology exam, he will still refer to him as Boner, even if they are opposing counsels working on a high-profile court case.

How to create a nickname

Step 1: Study your subject carefully to identify any physical quirks. If he is small consider Titch, if he has big ears Dumbo might be appropriate. Move to Step 2 if there are no obvious imperfections to ridicule.

Step 2: Assess his full name. Have his parents burdened him with an amusing set of initials? For example, Sam Trevor Ingle (STI) may evolve into Philis. Or, is it possible to compound his first and last name into a hilarious new word? Steve Hitchens becomes Shitchens and eventually Shits. Mike Hunt does not enjoy school.

Step 3: When neither of the above are applicable, suffixes in the form of 'y', 'ers' or 'zza' can be used to replace the last few letters of a surname, thus Windle becomes Windy, Madison becomes Madders and Lester becomes Lezza. This is the most common and least imaginative breed of nickname and is often used loudly when males are engaging in banter (see page 16).

Step 4: Superseding all other nicknames are those earned following public embarrassment, because a nickname with a back story is always better. Vomit on a school trip and you will forever be known as Spewy Chunkins – later, simply, Chunks.

Map-reading

A man's relationship with the map begins at around the same time he starts going to Scouts and/or reading fantasy novels. At Scouts he learns that it is a powerful travel tool that must be kept in a waterproof envelope at all times – he will spend many hours staring at it in a damp field wondering why, if it's so powerful, it is always sending him in the wrong direction. At home he charts Frodo's course through Middle Earth using

the illustrated maps of *The Lord of the Rings*, forever associating cartography with mystery, adventure and the romantic notion that a hobbit may be dwelling in the unmarked areas of a street atlas.

The fondness for maps, developed in childhood, endures into adulthood. This is why men would rather trust a 25-year-old *A–Z of Britain* that is missing several vital pages, and a brain that propelled them to a C in A-level Geography, than satnav.

To male drivers, a direction given by satnav isn't a statement of fact but the opening salvo in a frustrating dialogue concerning the wisdom of the suggested route. Even when the satnav has delivered him to his destination, the driver will insist it took him off the M5 a junction too early.

Which is a shame, because humanity has gone to a lot of trouble, spent a lot of money and utilised the brilliance of some of the planet's best scientists to put satellites into orbit that are capable of guiding an overpacked car to a holiday cottage in Cornwall.

How to use a map and compass

Step 1: Work out your location by identifying nearby landmarks on the map.

Step 2: Place the edge of your compass in a line from your starting to your finishing point, making sure the direction-of-travel arrow points towards your destination.

Step 3: Assess whether the direct route is the best option. If it involves tightly packed contour lines it means you might have to climb a mountain.

Step 4: If you decide to change your route, revisit Step 2 and plot a course around the mountain.

Step 5: Rotate the compass housing until the orienting arrow is parallel with the north–south lines on the map, pointing north.

Step 6: The number on the compass housing that aligns with the direction-of-travel arrow is your grid bearing. You must now add the magnetic declination/variation to this bearing, rotating the compass housing accordingly to accommodate the fact that magnetic north is always moving. The magnetic declination can be found in the map's Legend section.

Step 7: Turn the whole compass until the magnetic needle and the orienting arrow point in the same direction.

Step 8: Follow the direction-of-travel arrow.

Metal detecting

It's a sad indictment of the film industry that more Hollywood blockbusters are made about pirates than about metal-detecting enthusiasts, since, essentially, they are doing the same thing: hunting for treasure.

As well as the potential riches involved in both pursuits, pirates and metal-detecting enthusiasts are seduced by the escapism and romance associated with, respectively, a life on the high seas and a muddy field in Staffordshire.

Misplaced seriousness

There are many serious men in the world and many reasons to be serious. Unfortunately most serious men are serious about the wrong things, such as sport and jazz music.

To be fair, football can have life-or-death consequences if you find yourself in a particularly tight spot with an irate set of fans. But, obviously, these fans shouldn't be taking it so seriously.

Perhaps worse than being kicked into a coma by a group of men who are more upset by their team's poor form than world hunger, is being cornered by a jazz aficionado at a party and berated for owning a Michael Bublé album but never having heard of Thelonious Monk.

'Whenever a man does a thoroughly stupid thing, it is always from the noblest motives.'

Oscar Wilde

N
is for ...

Nail biting

When a man is biting his nails at least you know his fingers aren't picking his nose or scratching his scrotum; always reassuring. Of all the bad habits it is one of the least reprehensible and can be safely performed at work, thus saving the biter the bother of using a nail trimmer at home on his own time.

One of the main reasons men take up yoga is so they can still reach their toenails with their mouths at the age of thirty. So if you ever catch a man with part of his foot between his teeth, don't assume he is indulging in an auto-erotic act.

Nitpicking

Finding fault is one of man's favourite pastimes. If modern man had been hanging around as the final touches were being applied to the Palace of Westminster, he would have congratulated everybody concerned on the fine architecture but noted what a nightmare Gothic stone facades are to keep clean and how expensive the building would be to heat.

On a domestic level this can prove infuriating. What's the point of making an effort for someone if the first thing he comments on is the fact you've left a light on upstairs?

'Like all young men I set out to be a genius, but mercifully laughter intervened.'

Lawrence Durrell

Not sending Christmas cards

Christmas cards are a colossal waste of time and paper. Why, a man reasons, bother writing and posting one when the recipient will engage with it for a maximum of thirty seconds before standing it behind the intense nativity scene sent by Auntie Dorothy?

He also knows sending cards is a lifelong burden – once a reciprocal exchange is established, stopping out of the blue will leave the other side of the arrangement wondering what he has done to offend. And at Christmas, too.

That's not a commitment a man wants to make. Instead, from the moment he leaves home and his name drops off the family card, he will simply wait until he is in a long-term relationship and she starts adding him to hers.

Not staying in touch

There comes a point in almost every middle-aged man's life when he wonders why he hasn't got any friends. It's rarely because he is deeply unlikeable – the most unlikeable people tend to think they are extremely popular – and he will certainly know other men. Colleagues and his children's friends' parents will give him a day-to-day sense of belonging, but making the difficult transition from acquaintance to confidant is beyond all but the most sophisticated of social movers.

What he lacks is the well of shared experiences and mutually understood asides that a group of friends formed at school or university can fall back on. By contrast, he seems to spend most weekends visiting his other half's cohort of buddies who all met on the first day of nursery.

A man doesn't set out to lose contact with all the people who defined his early adulthood. He meanders there, periodically stopping to think: 'I must organise a weekend of real ale and cow tipping with the lads', but then fails to get around to it for so long that when he finally does, 'the lads' respond with emails beginning: 'I'm sorry who is this?'

O
is for ...

Obstacle course fanaticism

For some men, getting from A to B successfully without tripping over a paving stone or spilling coffee on their trousers isn't enough. They feel the need to prove they can also get from A to B by crawling along submerged tunnels, climbing over walls, wading through mud and running over hot coals, sometimes while wearing ridiculously impractical fancy dress.

Overdoing jokes

If a joke made you laugh once, a man is inclined to repeat it again and again, day after day after day until you tell him: 'IT'S NOT FUNNY ANY MORE.'

Overestimating DIY capabilities

There are three types of DIYer:

1) The pessimist – he will take one look at any job requiring practical knowhow and assume he doesn't have the right tools and it will take him days, if not months, to finish. He will react to a request to hang a picture in the same way he would to being sentenced to 350 hours community service.

2) The proficient – he has all the right tools and knows what to buy if he hasn't. He has built up his DIY expertise during years of patient practice. This is the rarest kind of DIYer.

3) The optimist – he doesn't have any of the necessary tools but will assume he can get the job done anyway. His favourite phrase, often uttered while holding a hammer and looking at the boiler, is: 'It'll be fine.'

The optimist is the most dangerous type and is responsible for nearly all emergency bank holiday call-outs to plumbers. He has a cavalier attitude to supporting walls and the location of live electric wiring and will, without fail, underestimate the time it takes to tile a bathroom. Any skills he hasn't been taught will, he is sure, simply emerge while he is on the job because of his innate practical sensibility.

How to put up a shelf

Step 1: Avoid areas of wall that are in a vertical or horizontal line with sockets and plugs to limit your chances of drilling through electrical wiring. If you think there may be plumbing in the vicinity, check using an electronic wire and pipe detector.

Step 2: If you are fixing the shelf to a stud wall, locate its timber studs by tapping the plasterboard surface (see Tapping on walls, page 186) or using a stud detector. Fix the brackets to the studs to ensure the shelf's life isn't a short one.

Step 3: Use a pencil to mark on the wall where you would like the shelf and brackets to go. Use a spirit level to make sure the line between the two brackets isn't a steep slope.

Step 4: Hold one bracket to the wall, check it is vertical, and make a mark in each fixing hole. Do the same with the second bracket.

Step 5: Drill holes for the brackets. If you are drilling into a masonry wall you will need a masonry drill bit and a drill with a 'hammer' setting. You will also need wall plugs that match the size of your screws.

Step 6: Screw the brackets into place, the longest arm of each bracket should be flat against the wall.

Step 7: Lay the shelf on the brackets and mark the location of the fixing holes. Remove the shelf and drill pilot holes over your markings.

Step 8: Lay it back on the brackets and fix into place using screws that are shorter than the height of the shelf. When stacking your shelf ask small children to stand well back to avoid injury in the event of collapse.

Overfilling pockets

Man bags may have tiptoed their way into acceptability but men would, on the whole, still rather go about their day-to-day business unencumbered by luggage, especially if that luggage could be misconstrued as a handbag. Unfortunately, the modern rage for tiny portable possessions has had the unexpected consequence of giving us more to carry.

In the old days a man went off to work clutching a piece of bread slathered in dripping and wrapped in waxy paper, with a threepenny bit in his pocket to pay for a post-shift beer, horse-and-carriage home and a pie. If he had also wanted to carry with him his entire music collection, his gramophone, his telephone, his address book and all the cash in his bank account, he would have needed a wheelbarrow, so he didn't bother.

Today, in one form or another, these have all been shrunk into portable gadgets – smartphones, mp4 players, headphones, debit cards and so on. Individually each one slips snugly into a pocket but collectively they form a seam-stretching bundle that gives the impression you have oddly inflamed upper thighs, leaving little room for a handkerchief.

Overuse of condiments

There is no meal that can't be improved by one of the many half-opened hot sauces and chutneys that take up at least three shelves in the average man's fridge.

P

is for ...

Packing the car

Arranging objects in the boot of a car isn't just a great opportunity for a man to demonstrate his spatial-reasoning skills. It's also a useful way of dodging the more stressful activities that precede a holiday, such as getting the kids ready, clearing the fridge of decomposing vegetable matter and finding passports.

How to pack the car

Step 1: Check the Maximum Permitted Weight (MPW) of your car in the handbook. Try not to exceed this.

Step 2: Clear the boot and footwells of unnecessary items – the spare tyre is not an unnecessary item.

Step 3: Pack the largest and heaviest items first, pushing them tightly against the back of the rear seat.

Step 4: Wedge smaller items around the larger items but always try and leave a relatively clear path to the spare tyre or tyre repair kit.

Step 5: Assess whether the driver can see out of the rear window. Ideally a car boot should not be packed higher than the top line of the rear seat backs, leaving

sightlines clear and preventing items from shooting forward if your vehicle stops suddenly.

Step 6: If necessary, remove items from the boot and put them in the rear passenger footwells. Never use the front footwells, especially the driver's, to stow luggage.

Step 7: Leave enough room for passengers in the rear to sit safely and comfortably. Do not pack heavy objects around children – in the event of an accident one or the other is likely to get damaged.

Step 8: Clear loose objects that could become potentially lethal projectiles from the parcel shelf.

Step 9: Refer to your car's handbook for the correct tyre pressure when carrying a full load. Inflate or deflate your tyres accordingly.

Step 10: Investigate the cost of a roof rack and car box.

Pessimism

There are men who always find the downside to a situation – going for a picnic? Looks like rain. Bought a house? In this market! Off travelling? There'll be no jobs when you get back. They have programmed themselves to expect disappointment so that when it arrives it will be balanced out by the joy of being proved right.

Petrol price chasing

A man may live next door to a petrol station but will happily drive twenty minutes down the road if this means he can save 1p a litre.

On long journeys he engages in a high-wire game of petrol price chasing, convinced the next set of pumps will supply fuel at a reduced rate that is entirely out of step with all the others he has passed. When he realises the car is dangerously close to giving up in the middle of a dual carriageway he will be forced to stop at the nearest station. Inevitably, this will be the most expensive.

Precise petrol-tank filling

Once he has selected his petrol station a man will attempt to fill his tank with an amount of fuel that costs a round number of pounds and pence. He will stop filling at £29.83, start again, stop again, start again, then overshoot to £30.03.

Filling up with exactly £30 of fuel brings no benefit whatsoever, but a man experiences few moments of genuine triumph during his day and takes great satisfaction in such small victories.

'Monkeys are superior to men in this: when a monkey looks into a mirror, he sees a monkey.'

Malcolm de Chazal

Poor social planning

There are very few things a man believes need careful planning: wars, public transport and tea breaks are among them. A social life isn't.

He lives by the maxim that 'the best nights are never planned', which is true if you are a student and every night involves going to the bar. Once you have left shared accommodation the chances all your friends will find themselves in the same place at the same time, all equally eager to get smashed, without a little pre-planning, are slim.

Still, he would rather keep his options open than commit to a dinner party three months in advance – who knows what he'll be in the mood for then? Probably not a dinner party. Especially if it involves bridging the conversation between an old university friend who was a campus celebrity thanks to his ability to burp the *Match of the Day* theme tune, and his wife's new boss.

How to host a stress-free dinner party

Step 1: Choose your guests carefully. Make sure some already know each other so that you aren't forced to initiate conversation all night.

Step 2: Ask about specific dietary requirements before you devise your menu.

Step 3: Plan a straightforward meal you can prepare, at least partly, in advance, that won't keep you in the kitchen for the entire evening (see How to cook a simple but impressive meal, page 105).

Step 4: Make sure you know exactly how long it takes to cook each dish. Nobody wants to be sitting down for the main course at 11pm, unless they are Spanish.

Step 5: Create an inoffensive dinner party playlist. This is not the time to introduce friends to avant-garde Scandinavian heavy metal.

Step 6: Add further atmosphere by dimming lamps and lighting candles.

Step 7: If you are hosting a large dinner party – more than eight people – create a table plan to prevent guests from milling about, refusing to commit to a place. And ensure established friends do not monopolise a certain area.

Step 8: Even if you think you have seasoned the food perfectly, always put salt and pepper on the table. And don't be upset if someone uses them.

Step 9: Never start the washing up until all guests have left. You do not want to give the impression you'd rather have clean plates than a good time. But clear away the worst of the mess before you go to bed – it'll make the morning after much more bearable.

Step 10: Do not run out of booze ...

Step 11: ... But when you start feeling tired, tell everybody you've run out of booze. They will soon leave.

Practising golf swings with an imaginary club

Every golf-playing man carries an imaginary bag of clubs with him at all times. When he has a spare moment, or is left awkwardly standing on his own at a wedding, he will take out one of those clubs, form a grip around its handle and start swishing it back and forth.

It is a comfort blanket that reminds him of his happy place – the fairway. The same applies to imaginary cricket bats. He may also, on occasion, shimmy around a lamp post holding a non-existent rugby ball. In all cases he is much more proficient at imaginary sport than real sport.

(See also: Air drumming, page 6)

Pretending to swallow cutlery

Up to the age of four children are genuinely beguiled by men who appear capable of swallowing cutlery. Sadly, they're less impressed when their father bounds into the room during their fifteenth birthday party, tilts his head back and slides a spoon down the side of his face.

Purchasing power tools

Dad may only be constructing a run for his child's guinea pig, but why use a handsaw to cut the necessary pieces of timber when there are shops selling petrol-powered pneumatic chainsaws capable of slicing through concrete? After all, although it's unlikely, he may one day be asked to dismantle a car park.

> **'But lo! men have become the tools of their tools.'**
>
> *Henry David Thoreau*

Putting a finger in the wind

The ability to identify which way the wind is blowing simply by licking a finger is a skill that sons pick up by watching their fathers and grandfathers erecting windbreaks on the beach and deciding where to light campfires.

It is a technique that is rendered near pointless by its many flaws – it relies on the ability to detect a small drop in temperature on one side of your finger, not to mention the annoying habit wind has of changing direction – but since when has flawed logic ever stopped a man?

Punning

Men who regularly resort to puns are eager to demonstrate their verbal dexterity to those around them. Handily, a pun will also divert attention until a man has something genuinely witty or useful to say about the matter in hand.

Twitter has revolutionised the life of the punning man, allowing him to pun competitively twenty-four hours a day by latching on to relevant trending hashtags – #cheesyfilms or #fishybands, for instance – to come up with gems like: Full Feta Jacket, The Paneer Hunter, Dire Baits and Salmon and Garfunkeel.

'The worst men often give the best advice.'

Francis Bacon

Q

is for...

Questioning expert advice

An expert opinion is there to be questioned. The moment British Gas pop round and condemn a man's boiler as unsafe he will immediately dispute this, based on the fact he is not dead.

Perhaps the expert a man ignores most during his, probably short, lifetime is his doctor, who spends their relationship lecturing him on the merits of fruit and vegetables and the dangers of overindulging in alcohol and red meat. Especially since the only exercise he takes involves walking to the shop to stock up on pork scratchings.

He is unlikely to follow this advice until old ladies start overtaking him on stairs and offering to help him cross the road. In response he will develop a joint-shattering triathlon obsession. The doctor will advise against this.

Quizzes

Who needs Wikipedia when you have a man's brain to hand? Quizzes of all varieties, especially those in pubs that come with beer, provide him with an opportunity to unleash the vast tome of facts that lies unused behind his forehead.

Despite this huge intellectual resource, the common male reaction to a quiz question involves clawing at his hair and muttering 'I know this one'. Which isn't strictly true, since a vital part of knowing an answer is being able to supply it when the relevant question is asked. The situation will resolve itself in one of two ways:

1) He will question the validity of the question vehemently. When he eventually fails to win the quiz he will leave the pub frustrated by the knowledge that had the right questions been asked he would have known the answers.

2) He will pretend he has an important phone call to make before going outside and finding the answer on Wikipedia.

Of course there's one thing worse than being beaten by a cheat and that's being beaten by someone who knows it all.

Quoting films

Men who sprinkle their conversation with film quotes live under the misapprehension that repeating a vaguely relevant line from *Monty Python's Life of Brian* will leave their audience amused and in awe. Unfortunately, for every person who smiles knowingly, 38,000 will have no idea what they are talking about.

They tend to prefer quotes that hint at a cultured taste in film. Or make them sound really hard. Here are some favourites:

'You're a big man, but you're in bad shape'
– Michael Caine in *Get Carter*

'You talkin' to me? You talkin' to me? You talkin' to me? Then who the hell else are you talking ... you talking to me? Well I'm the only one here'
– Robert De Niro in *Taxi Driver*

'You've got to ask yourself one question: "Do I feel lucky?" Well, do you, punk?'
– Clint Eastwood in *Dirty Harry*

'Get busy living, or get busy dying'
– Tim Robbins in *The Shawshank Redemption*

'He's not the Messiah. He's a very naughty boy!'
– Terry Jones in *Monty Python's Life of Brian*

'I'm as mad as hell, and I'm not gonna take this anymore!'
– Peter Finch in *Network*

'We want the finest wines available to humanity. And we want them here, and we want them now!'
– Richard E. Grant in *Withnail & I*

'That rug really tied the room together'
– John Goodman in *The Big Lebowski*

'I coulda had class. I coulda been a contender. I coulda been somebody'
– Marlon Brando in *On the Waterfront*

'The Force is strong with this one'
– James Earl Jones *in Star Wars: Episode IV – A New Hope*

R is for ...

Rearranging testicles

Often referred to euphemistically as 'rearranging the furniture', even though very few pieces of furniture resemble male genitalia.

If a testicle finds itself trapped on the wrong side of a pair of briefs; entangled horrifically in a pair of twisted boxer shorts; sweatily clinging to a thigh or, for no obvious reason, is a little uncomfortable, a man will have no choice but to take immediate action. Even if he is about to shake hands with the Queen.

'A man who does not think for himself does not think at all.'

Oscar Wilde

Refusal to admit they are crying

It's OK for men to cry in certain scenarios: at funerals, during a child's first nativity play, or while watching *Ghost*. But a man will still resist, contorting his features and chewing his lips so desperately it appears his face is involved in a fight with itself.

Coping with difficult situations stoically is a peculiar British tradition which commonly results in men choosing to internalise emotional pain and prolong it, rather than have a good cry and start feeling better.

Epochal moments in our history are used to reinforce this national personality trait. Some say the Second World War would never have been won without Britain's collective stiff upper lip. Although Americans and Russians may beg to differ, it's certainly true hysterics were not the done thing during a heavy bombing raid.

Attitudes have softened slightly since, but if a man cries in full puffy-faced glory more than once a year he will invariably be greeted with a 'what is wrong with him this time?' roll of the eyes.

Relationship laziness

In the early days of a relationship a man will try and convince his new love interest that he's the kind of guy who showers once a day, can cook lasagne without referring to a recipe and enjoys prolonged love-making sessions involving massages and fruit. However, it doesn't take long for his multitalented, metrosexual mask to slip, leaving his true I'd-rather-stay-in-and-watch-the-football-with-a-takeaway face on display.

The effort he puts into a relationship is inversely proportional to the amount of time he spends with his girlfriend. When a couple stop referring to time together as a 'date', because they spend more time together than apart, it is a warning sign that his urge to impress is fading. Once cohabiting begins, the chances of him spontaneously organising a riverside bike ride and picnic drop significantly.

This shouldn't be read as an indication that he no longer cares – in fact, it's a sign he is content. Men are at their most comfortable when they are, literally, at their most comfortable: on the sofa, watching TV in a room with someone they don't have to make polite conversation with who may, on occasion, give them a blow job. Why book a table at Pizza Express if you've got everything you need at home?

'Men do not fail; they give up trying.'

Elihu Root

Road rage

The Highway Code is pretty clear on most matters: you must not exceed the speed limit; you must stop at a red light; you must not drive on the hard shoulder unless it is an emergency, and so on.

In theory this should make the nation's roads a straightforward place to be, where everybody follows the same rules and gets along fine – just like in North Korea. Unfortunately, a man armed with the certainty of rules – which obviously don't apply as rigorously to him as they do to everybody else – is a dangerous beast, especially when he is cocooned from the rest of humanity in a fast-moving metal box. It doesn't help that shows such as *Top Gear* have spread the notion that it is every man's right to drive exactly how he likes. Ideally in a pair of jeans that are indecently tight around the groin area.

The belief that the law is on his side gives a man licence to mouth 'wanker' at anybody who ventures into the middle lane of the motorway and isn't driving at 90mph; throw his hands up towards the sky in utter, utter despair when the driver in front moves a little slowly off a junction; and wish death upon anybody who dares to stop in a yellow box. And not a peaceful, in-your-sleep kind of death.

Of course, no man has read the *Highway Code* since he passed his test, leaving them all operating under a patchy set of rules consisting of the ones they remember and the ones they don't think are stupid. This is why two men separated by nothing but a car door can form fiercely opposing interpretations of the same road-traffic situation and get so very angry about it.

'Men are like steel. When they lose their temper, they lose their worth.'

Chuck Norris

Role playing

Role playing means different things to different men. To some it involves roaming around a forest, possibly wearing an orc mask and holding a latex axe, as part of an elaborate fantasy game. This is known as live action role play, or LARP to insiders.

To others role playing involves pretending to be a high-powered chief executive, picking up a woman (his wife) in a bar and taking her to a hotel room where he has an excuse to engage in acts he's not usually allowed to, such as drinking from the mini bar and light bondage.

It's rare for these two forms of role play to overlap – mainly because posh cocktail joints make you leave axes at the door. Either way role playing usually features sex or violence. Two of man's favourite things.

How to win at sexy role play

Step 1: Discuss your fantasies with your partner to find out where there is some common ground.

Step 2: If one of you is more reticent than the other, always work within his or her limits. Save the dungeon for later.

Step 3: Take your role playing out of the family home if you have children to avoid any troubling questions.

Step 4: Start slowly with a scenario that puts you both at ease such as strangers meeting in a hotel bar, as described opposite.

Step 5: Play with the dynamics of your relationship, swapping submissive and dominant roles.

Step 6: Introduce something new into your bedroom routine. This could be a sensual massage, an unfamiliar sexual position or a spanking paddle.

Step 7: Agree a safe word which allows either of you to opt out at any moment.

Step 8: Afterwards, reassure your partner it is her dressed as a policewoman you find sexy, not all policewomen in general.

R

Running in a half-arsed manner

Men don't like to amble. Ambling suggests they have nowhere important to be and, even if they haven't, that's not the image they want to portray. Unfortunately, breaking into a sprint on a busy pavement isn't always practical.

Bounding is an option, but this only comes naturally to generals and those who are used to striding across country estates from a young age. The long stride of the bounder also reduces his ability to agilely sidestep the moving obstacles that clutter the modern pedestrian environment, such as children on scooters or, worse, adults on scooters.

In most cases, when a chap feels the urge to run in this situation he inhibits his natural instinct, leaving him in a locomotive no man's land in which his legs start to jog while his upper body continues to walk. This gait also occurs at pelican crossings if he steps into the road just as the green man starts to flash.

S

is for ...

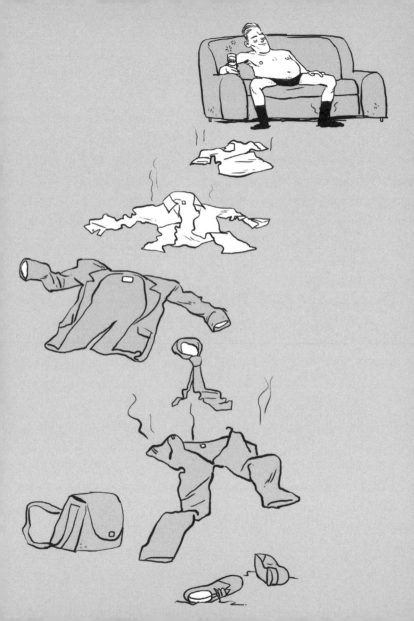

Scattering sweaty clothes

When a heavily perspiring man walks through his front door – usually after intense exercise or a particularly humid commute – he will immediately start taking his clothes off. He does this with every intention of putting them into the dirty laundry basket once he has cooled down and had a shower. Sadly, once he has cooled down and had a shower he really doesn't feel like picking them up, not until he's had a sit-down and a beer, anyway.

Ideally, rather than leaving a sweaty garment trail as he moves around the house, he would put his clothes directly in the washing machine. In a utopian world he would then add more dirty washing of the same colour to create a full load. And turn the machine on.

In reality he will simply drop his damp squash kit into the laundry basket, think 'job done' and let it fester for a couple of days until an unlucky soul – obviously not him – reaches in and grabs a handful of his putrefying socks.

Silence

Male friendships aren't based on the ability to effortlessly chat for hours and hours, they're based on the ability to sit comfortably in silence together. A man's best friends are those he doesn't have talk to, which is why his best friend is often a dog – an animal it is almost impossible to have an awkward silence with.

It's important to keep a safe distance when attempting a comfortable silence. Only lovers and strangers on overcrowded Tube trains are able to sit with their legs touching and not find themselves overcome with anxiety.

'Blessed is the man who, having nothing to say, abstains from giving us wordy evidence of the fact.'

George Eliot

Sitting on the loo

If you are a man, most visits to the bathroom involve standing over a toilet (see Inaccurate peeing, page 86), which makes sitting on one something of a novelty. This is why men like to savour the moment. It is not uncommon for a man to read a book or newspaper before, during and after his bowel movement, often extending his stay to haemorrhoid-inducing lengths. But that's a small price to pay for twenty uninterrupted minutes with the sports section.

Some people encourage house guests to read on the toilet by providing a basket of magazines and novelty books. If you are tempted to pick one up just have a think about the last person who read that particular issue of *House & Home* and what they were doing. Can you be sure he stopped reading before he started wiping?

The smartphone has added a new dimension to sitting on the loo, allowing people to conduct their business while ... doing their business. It has also prompted one of the most pressing questions of our time: is it ever OK to answer the phone while having a poo?

UHN-

Skimming stones

Take a stroll along a shingle beach and, among the jellyfish corpses and incongruous flotsam and jetsam, you are likely to find a man skimming stones.

He might be alone, lost in an attempt to beat the unwitnessed 23er he scored one morning in Bognor Regis. He might be with friends trying to convince them he once scored a 23er in Bognor Regis. Or he might be accompanied by children, rapt by his ability to trick a stone into skipping across the water's surface.

These children will attempt to follow him, selecting unsuitably large stones of their own and hurling them directly into the oncoming waves again and again, bamboozled by his logic-confounding sorcery. Some will lose interest, others will continue selecting and throwing, selecting and throwing, selecting and throwing, until eventually they decipher the mystery, and a skimmer is born.

It's usually a boy, since boys are, on the whole, prepared to devote more time to mastering skills that serve no purpose other than to demonstrate their physical

How to skim a stone

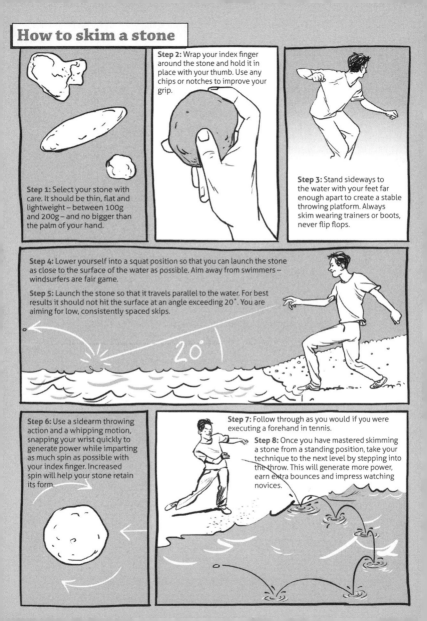

Step 1: Select your stone with care. It should be thin, flat and lightweight – between 100g and 200g – and no bigger than the palm of your hand.

Step 2: Wrap your index finger around the stone and hold it in place with your thumb. Use any chips or notches to improve your grip.

Step 3: Stand sideways to the water with your feet far enough apart to create a stable throwing platform. Always skim wearing trainers or boots, never flip flops.

Step 4: Lower yourself into a squat position so that you can launch the stone as close to the surface of the water as possible. Aim away from swimmers – windsurfers are fair game.

Step 5: Launch the stone so that it travels parallel to the water. For best results it should not hit the surface at an angle exceeding 20°. You are aiming for low, consistently spaced skips.

20°

Step 6: Use a sidearm throwing action and a whipping motion, snapping your wrist quickly to generate power while imparting as much spin as possible with your index finger. Increased spin will help your stone retain its form.

Step 7: Follow through as you would if you were executing a forehand in tennis.

Step 8: Once you have mastered skimming a stone from a standing position, take your technique to the next level by stepping into the throw. This will generate more power, earn extra bounces and impress watching novices.

superiority. Skimming stones is particularly suited to this; it can be measured easily, you simply have to count the skips and round the figure up (everybody else will), allowing a group of skimmers to form an impromptu league table and shower the least able with soul-crushing banter (see Banter, page 16).

Skin-to-skin bonding with babies

These days a child barely draws his first breath before he is wrenched away from the comforting bosom of his mother and forced to confront the wobbling upper body of his semi-naked father. As if midwives didn't have enough to deal with already, they are now expected to carry out their duties knowing that, at any moment, they could turn around and be confronted by a nascent pair of moobs.

The more discrete dad will deposit his newborn baby under his t-shirt, where he will spend the early minutes of his life being poked in the face by wiry chest hairs. Pictures of the moment will be shared immediately to prove that he is a thoroughly modern father who would, under no circumstances, have preferred to be in the pub during the muckier bits of childbirth.

Spreading out

Like gas, a man will always expand to fill the space available. On public transport and in cinemas he will monopolise the armrest and legroom areas, given the opportunity. If you share a bed with a man and have more than a 2in sliver of mattress to work with by morning he is either an abnormally still sleeper or has passed away in the night.

Sulking about football results

The football-loving man invests huge amounts of emotional, and actual, capital into following his favourite team. If that team loses it makes him very unhappy, often to the point that he refuses to talk to his wife and children no matter how hard they argue that that last-minute penalty wasn't entirely their fault.

Unfortunately, the nature of the sport dictates that most teams are unsuccessful most of the time. Yet a fervent fan is compelled to continue watching his team no matter how poorly they perform. Each depressing loss is therefore followed by the depressing realisation that he'll have to go through it all again next weekend. Possibly after a six-hour drive to Middlesbrough.

Few forms of entertainment involve quite such a level of self-flagellation. Imagine going to a twenty-screen multiplex cinema every Saturday and being forced to sit through a Steven Seagal film each time.

When a fan can't get to a game he will commit his Saturday afternoon to watching results shows on TV that consist of former professional players watching matches on his behalf and describing the action. Badly. Sometimes he will listen to a match on the radio at the same time.

Such devotion does have its upsides, though. The football fan has built up a depth of knowledge that he can call on at any time, often, and most usefully, to make conversation with other men at social events he'd rather not have been invited to.

Partners with no interest in the sport will be amazed by their other half's ability to recall Norwich City's longest ever unbeaten run. Especially since he failed to remember their wedding anniversary last month and, just yesterday, went to the shop for some kitchen roll only to return with six cloudy stouts, a family pack of chocolate buttons and a roll of cling film.

Stretching

A man standing on one foot, clutching the other against a buttock, or pushing against a wall with one leg straightened diagonally behind him is caught in the middle of a profound battle against his own physical decay, otherwise known as stretching.

Men over the age of thirty who continue to play sport exist in a permanent state of slight pain, their ossifying tendons and muscles aggravated by the merest hint of strenuous movement. When a heel swells or a hamstring tightens they hobble to the internet in search of answers. Inevitably the answer is a complicated series of yogic manoeuvres that must be repeated five times a day.

Depressingly, once one part of the body has been stretched back into working order another unravels. It is a battle he can never win.

Surfing

Men used to treat a visit to the British coast as an opportunity to eat cockles and stare at the sea from a bus shelter. Now they're stripping off in car parks in the middle of winter, hauling on wetsuits, talking earnestly about rip tides and swells and wrestling surfboards across gale-buffeted beaches.

The curiosity that prompts a man to sign up for a surfing lesson during a family holiday in Cornwall morphs into an obsession, despite his persistent lack of improvement, when he becomes hooked on the simplicity of life amid the waves. The troubles of a modern existence drift away and he is left with just two very clearly defined tasks: try to catch a wave and try not to die.

T

is for ...

Tapping on walls

The ability to identify the inner workings of a wall simply by tapping on it with your knuckles and translating the timbre of the tap into actual knowledge, is a skill, similar to bleeding radiators (see page 28), that is relatively easy to get the hang of, but a befuddling mystery to those who have never tried it.

Understanding whether you're dealing with a supporting wall or a stud wall has immense practical benefits. For example, it will prevent you accidentally demolishing your house when carrying out amateur renovations or attempting to nail a picture hook into 3ft-thick, 300-year-old stone. It also ensures a man will never be stuck for something to do as long as he has a wall to hand, which is why he can sometimes be seen tapping one while queuing for the bathroom at parties. 'That's an internal stud, they've probably put the plumbing through there,' he'll be thinking.

How to hang an item on a stud wall

Step 1: Bear in mind studs are around 1.5in wide and are usually spaced 16in apart, although this may vary in older homes.

Step 2: Look for clues to help you locate a stud that can be used as a reference point: mounting boxes for sockets and plugs are often attached to the side of timber studs; visible nailheads are also a sign that plasterboard has been fixed to a stud in that location.

Step 3: Alternatively, work from the stud situated where the wall forms a corner in the room.

Step 4: Measure in 16in increments from the centre of your reference stud to the position you would like to fix an item to the wall.

Step 5: Tap the wall with your knuckles to confirm the presence of a stud. A low thud indicates that you have found one; a hollow echo indicates there is nothing behind the plasterboard but thin air.

Step 6: Drill a small hole, remembering never to drill into a stud that electrical outlets are fixed to. If the drill bit meets resistance beyond the plasterboard you have hit the stud.

Step 7: If it doesn't, insert a long thin nail in the hole at an angle to locate the stud edge. Drill another hole, about three-quarters of an inch from the edge, to find the centre.

Step 8: Fill in and paint over the redundant holes you have created. Hang the item.

Television shows about sharks

Of all the fish, if a man had to choose, he'd like to be a shark – they don't say much, but their awesome power and athletic killing ability command respect among their aquatic peers. Strangely, the manatee doesn't excite such interest despite its more enlightened, non-violent approach to life.

Natural history channels understand this and devote around half their scheduling to television shows that involve a gnarled man-of-the-sea cajoling, coaxing, poking and provoking a great white until it starts chewing reluctantly on his shark cage as an excited voiceover exclaims: 'Out of nowhere the eighteen-foot killing machine attacked. At any minute everybody could die horrifically.'

Film-makers who work closely with sharks claim the species is misunderstood and its threat to humanity overdramatised, yet proceed to make documentaries entitled 'Apocalypse Shark: Mega Fish Attack!'

'I believe implicitly that every young man in the world is fascinated with either sharks or dinosaurs.'

Peter Benchley

Turning everything into a competition

Life is a competition. From birth babies are charted; although this is simply to monitor their growth, parents are delighted when they break into the seventy-fifth centile. In school, college and university, children and young adults are encouraged to beat their peers academically and on the sporting field. At work, ambition is lauded and promotion above colleagues celebrated.

Men are incapable of switching this competitive spirit off in their spare time, which is why they find satisfaction in being able to down a pint of mildly poisonous liquid – lager – faster than their friends and can never refuse an invitation to arm wrestle (see page 14).

U

is for ...

Undressing in public

Young men are particularly fond of public nudity. On hot days they can be seen walking through town centres topless, t-shirts tucked into their jeans and flapping about their legs. This is understandable – it's hot and their stomachs are still flat – although not a freedom granted to their female friends.

Students also enjoy taking their clothes off, especially those involved in sports clubs. Whether men inclined to public nudity are more likely to join sports clubs, or whether spending a lot of time naked together in a communal shower gives a man a more liberal attitude to public nudity, nobody is entirely sure. But on a night out, if the majority of the rugby team are still wearing trousers by 2 a.m. it is a surprise.

'A naked woman in heels is a beautiful thing. A naked man in shoes looks like a fool.'

Christian Louboutin

Underwhelming reactions

Christmas and birthdays are agony for the kind of man who finds exaggerated displays of emotion difficult. If he could he would take his presents away and open them in a room on his own with the door locked, before sending an email three weeks later to say thanks.

Unfortunately, he is forced to perform this painful tradition in front of an expectant audience of relatives who will inevitably feel slightly disappointed when he mumbles: 'That's great. Cheers', whether he unwraps a mug tree or the keys to a new Ferrari.

Unnecessary gadget accumulation

A 64in plasma television with 3D capability is good enough for anyone. Until a 64in plasma television with 3D capability and a voice recognition feature comes on to the market, at which point the gadget-hungry man suddenly feels like he has fallen behind the times. Anxious not to be laughed out of his own home by visiting friends, he will rush out to buy a TV he can hold a conversation with.

It is the same mentality that prompts him to set up camp outside an Apple shop several days before the release of a new iPhone that has a slightly bigger screen than the iPhone he queued up to buy last year.

'The real problem is not whether machines think but whether men do.'

B. F. Skinner

V

is for ...

Vaulting over low fences

Done properly, the fence vault is the most elegant way to exit a field known to man. A combination of power and coordination, it is an impressive act that every man wants in his armoury. By contrast, leaving a field over a stile invites all sorts of clumsy limb-related confusion; although better that than a stomach-crushing brush

with a kissing gate, a contraption clearly invented by a man who has never carried a rucksack. Or eaten.

However, the fence vault will make a fool of a man at some point in his life, either when he is young and overconfident, or old and carrying a hamstring strain. Catch a trouser leg on a section of barbed wire, or fail to clear the top batten with his feet, and the momentum of his upper body will force him into a humiliating, panic-inducing face-first dive.

Still, that's not enough to put him off, even though there are only two situations in which he will ever actually need to exit a field by vaulting a fence:

1) When he is surrounded by a herd of agitated cows.

2) When he is surrounded by a herd of agitated farmers, one of whom has a shotgun.

How to negotiate a herd of agitated cows safely

Step 1: Keep your dog on a leash – despite being ten times its size the cow views an unrestrained canine as a potent threat. However, if a cow should charge in your direction, release your pet to divert attention.

Step 2: Do not pat cows. Keep your distance, especially if there are calves present.

Step 3: Remain on the path; if you must walk through a herd make sure you do not startle the animals. Talking in a calm voice will alert cattle to your presence before you are too close.

Step 4: If you are in coastal areas do not put yourself between a herd and a cliff edge.

Step 5: Walk confidently through the herd, but do not run and never make direct eye contact with a cow.

Step 6: If one of the herd approaches aggressively, do not turn your back on it. Keep facing the animal as you edge out of the field and try not to make any sudden movements.

Step 7: As a last resort hit it sharply and precisely on the nose with a hiking stick.

Step 8: Always carry a hiking stick.

Very short phone conversations

If a telephone conversation with your father gets beyond: 'Hello, how are you?' before he mutters: 'Hang on, I'll get your mother', you should consider it a huge success. Men, especially older men, do not like talking on the phone unless there is a clear and specific practical reason to do so – to check when his daughter-in-law's birthday is, perhaps. And her name.

Such perfunctory communication isn't limited to the telephone. Emails focus on the job at hand, eschewing any hint of affection in a bid to save on virtual ink and paper:

```
Do you have some string I could borrow?
Dad
ps Sorry to hear about the divorce
```

He takes a similarly minimalist approach to birthday cards, relying on the manufacturer to express everything that needs to be said, apart from who the card is to and who it is from.

Voice volume-control issues

Some men mumble, some men talk as if they are attempting to outshout an idling passenger jet engine when they are nowhere near an idling passenger jet engine. Some men do both.

The mumbling man relays his thoughts at a volume just higher than the volume he is thinking them at. He is so engrossed in the thought process that he forgets to separate it from the speech process, to the extent it isn't really clear if he is speaking or thinking. Either that or he is so unsure of the worth of what he has to say he lacks the confidence to say it audibly. When nobody responds because they can't hear him, it reinforces his low opinion of his own opinions and perpetuates the vicious mumbling circle.

The man who talks loudly is searching for a deep-toned resonance that he thinks will add weight and authority to his words. You will often find men who talk loudly have very little to say.

The man who does both is attempting to compensate for one or the other, usually at the wrong time.

W

is for ...

War games

Since the mid twentieth century men in the West have, on the whole, been sheltered from the rigours of battle and have grown fond of a day-to-day existence that doesn't involve considerable bloodshed. But the warring instinct remains strong – paintballing and other games that mimic battle allow men to satisfy that instinct and live well into retirement.

Watching action films

The plot may be thinner than Jason Statham's hair, the acting would shame a fence post, but DID YOU SEE THAT MASSIVE EXPLOSION!

Wearing pointy shoes with jeans

Smart-casual is a difficult fashion trick to pull off – so difficult it is almost impossible and should be approached with extreme caution. The union of pointy shoes that elongate the foot to clownish lengths and jeans that are, understandably, distressed, is at the apex of a phenomenon that can be witnessed in nightclub queues across the nation every weekend.

If only bouncers weren't the arbiters of tasteful evening wear this might never have happened.

How to get into a nightclub

Step 1: Observe the nightclub's queue from a safe distance. Take notes: what are people wearing? How do they act? Are the door staff aloof or do they enjoy a chat? Do they only allow celebrities in?

Step 2: Taking your research into account, select your outfit. The appropriate attire will vary dramatically from club to club, but as a general rule those outside large cities do not welcome the combination of casual denim and trainers.

Step 3: Join the queue sober, or at least give the impression of sobriety. Despite their reputation bouncers are keen to avoid violence and drunk men are always the most eager, if least able, fighters.

Step 4: Split large groups into pairs. Bouncers have learnt that a pack of men in smart shirts is almost impossible to quell once it scents blood. Straight clubs like to maintain a gender balance so include a woman in each pair if you can.

Step 5: Approach door staff confidently and offer a brief greeting – 'evening' is effective here. If they decide to expand the conversation you may reciprocate, possibly dropping into conversation the name of a guest DJ playing that evening.

Step 6: Understand that on some occasions you will be denied entry simply because your face isn't quite right. Accept this irrational reasoning with grace and humility to avoid damaging your chances of getting in next time.

Wearing trainers with shorts

In Britain it is only warm enough to wander about with bare feet three days a year, which is why boys grow up wearing sensible shoes, comfortable trainers and wellington boots. Always accompanied, of course, by socks. It is only when they hit adulthood and spend a gap year mixing with exotic peoples who glide about in flip flops that they start to reassess their relationship with their feet.

Unfortunately, whereas a flip flop appears to have evolved into an extension of the Australian's body, to the British man it is a shoe without the best bits – laces, toecaps, a slight aroma of dampness, and so on – that attaches to his foot via a single strand of plastic that he must, ridiculously, hold between his toes.

This is all very well when shuffling from the pool to the communal pool toilets, but transforms longer walks into claw-toed, calf-muscle-cramping ordeals. A British man would prefer the indignity of wearing shorts with trainers and socks, a look that – if the shorts are very short – suggests he is about to go for a long run or tramp up a hill, or – if the shorts are long – that he's borrowed his lower legs from a dwarf.

'Great men are seldom over-scrupulous in the arrangement of their attire.'

Charles Dickens

Weather optimism

A man will let nothing come between him and his plans, especially not something as trifling as the weather which, as luck would have it, is always on the verge of 'clearing up'. This is why men insist on barbecuing in the rain and why it's generally men who feature in news reports about groups of underprepared climbers having to be airlifted out of

a blizzard by a mountain rescue helicopter. It is also why, even in the cloudiest of climates, men attach solar panels to their homes.

Whistling

There are three forms of whistling in common use: the melodic accompaniment to a practical task, the piercing two-fingers-in-mouth blast used to attract the attention of a dog or child, and the wolf whistle. All three are dying arts.

A man building a tree house is much less likely to entertain himself by whistling *The Great Escape* theme tune now it is possible to pipe a complex symphony into his ears. The ageing farming population and waning coverage of sheepdog trials on national television mean all the best two-fingered whistlers will be dead by 2050, and for those who remain there'll be an app that allows them to operate a border collie from their bedrooms. And men are gradually learning that wolf whistling isn't much more sophisticated than shouting 'PHWOAR' while rubbing their thighs and drooling.

Wine expertise

A man's relationship with wine goes through several distinct phases. When he starts his drinking career he views it as a middle-aged tipple that has no place in a teenage boy's hand. And why would it when there are beverages available that taste like Ribena and get you drunk?

At university beer is his staple, but he will splash out on red wine, candles and, possibly, a cravat, to impress the girls in his halls. By the time he has reached his mid to late twenties he is regularly buying bottles to drink at home and take to parties, he might even, on occasion, buy it in a pub. But never by the glass. That's worse than ordering half a pint.

He'll know he is truly on the way to middle age when he has identified a preferred grape variety and spends more than £5 on a bottle because he is beginning to prioritise flavour over intoxication. Although, naturally, getting pleasantly sloshed is still on his to-do list.

From here he rapidly develops into a self-certified wine authority. He will insist on swirling and noisily slurping it in restaurants and tut when one of his party dares pair a hearty Cabernet Sauvignon with delicate white-fleshed fish.

How to pair wine and food

Step 1: If time is of the essence simply assess the colour of the food you plan to cook and match it with a wine of similar hue. If it isn't move to Step 2.

Step 2: Unless you are cooking Lancashire hotpot, search for a vintage that originates from the same region as your dish since, in the first instance, wine was made to accompany food from the area in which it was produced.

Step 3: Balance the weight of food and wine. A lean crisp white such as a Muscadet complements salads and white fish; a weightier red Malbec suits steak and hard cheese. Wines with less alcohol tend to be lighter-bodied than their boozier brethren so, when creating a menu, bear in mind how drunk you would like to be by the end of the meal.

Step 4: Consider how ingredients have been cooked and the composition of the sauce that will accompany them. For example, a medium-bodied Pinot Noir works well with the spice of a chicken tikka masala when there is no lager to hand, whereas Chenin Blanc is a subtle accompaniment to chicken risotto.

Step 5: Emphasise the flavours in a dish by reflecting its ingredients in the wine's tasting notes. Quaff a grapey Muscat with fruit-based desserts, or a buttery oak barrel-aged Chardonnay with creamy sauces.

Step 6: Alternatively, contrast notes and flavours to enhance a meal. The sweetness of an off-dry wine will, for example, add balance to a fiery dish, while older wines boasting more complexity are best paired with simpler food.

Step 7: Impress/irritate your friends by explaining your wine choices in great detail over dinner.

W

'Wine hath drowned more men than the sea.'

Thomas Fuller

Wrestling old friends

Boys wrestle partly because of a primordial imperative to prove their alpha male credentials and partly because they have lots of energy and not much to talk about. In adulthood wrestling old friends is a way of showing affection without having to say anything embarrassing. But a man will only wrestle those friends he wrestled with as a boy – putting Simon from Accounts in a headlock just doesn't feel appropriate.

For some men the urge to demonstrate their alpha male status doesn't wane with age. These are the kinds of men who take up cage fighting for fun. If you know someone like this delete his number immediately, move home and provide a false forwarding address.

(See also: Arm wrestling, page 14)

How to escape a standing headlock

Step 1: Assuming your attacker is holding your head with his right arm, free your left arm then wrap it back and over his right shoulder.

Step 2: Push your left hand aggressively into his face. If he is not merely a playful old friend you may also want to poke your fingers into his eyes or nose.

Step 3: Place your right hand firmly on your attacker's left wrist to prevent him using this arm to strike you.

Step 4: While pushing into his face sweep your left leg forward and forcefully knee him behind his right knee.

Step 5: Drop your attacker to the ground and run.

Writing bad poetry

Young men often turn to poetry when they want to express love for a girl in upper sixth or rage against an unjust world. It is a noble art form and a far better use of time than swapping semi-naked selfies on Snapchat.

Writing poetry, however, isn't easy, even though some of the best poems fit together so naturally it seems absurd anybody would put the words in any other order. Most young men don't have the patience to craft verse that, even if they are essentially balanced and well-adjusted humans, doesn't read like it's been written by an unhinged ten-year-old.

X
is for ...

Xenophilia

There's nothing wrong with appreciating foreign cultures, really there isn't. But a man who looks in the mirror and sees a sophisticated fellow of worldly tastes usually can't resist letting the world know how worldly he is. A xenophile won't simply return from the Far East with some nice photos of snow monkeys, he will return with a kimono for every day of the week and insist on eating dinner kneeling on the floor. Even in Nando's.

'Nymphomaniac: a woman as obsessed with sex as an average man.'

Mignon McLaughlin

X-rated fantasies

Male sexual expectations have altered dramatically since copulation went digital (see page 220). Here's a quick look at the recent evolution of male fantasies.

1890s: Scullery maid drops silver spoon, as she leans down to pick it up she briefly reveals her left ankle.

1970s: Secretary takes her glasses off to reveal that she is, in fact, beautiful. She then works her way through *The Joy of Sex* – or at least the first chapter – with her boss.

2010s: Three maids stumble across two secretaries having sex with an inexplicably irresistible middle-aged man in a hotel room. Everybody has sex with each other and several saucily shaped objects.

As the complexity of male fantasies increases, the likelihood of them ever happening decreases. Mainly because, what with busy social calendars and all the after-school clubs the kids need taking to, it's really hard to get everybody in the same room at the same time. But also, if a man was actually presented with this scenario, he would be terrified.

He may ask his partner to have a Brazilian wax once in a while, though.

X-rated online viewing

Thanks to the internet we can now watch as much hardcore porn as our brains can handle, which is an opportunity men find particularly hard to pass up. Combined with another exciting development of the digital age, working from home, this has created the perfect masturbatory storm.

Y

is for ...

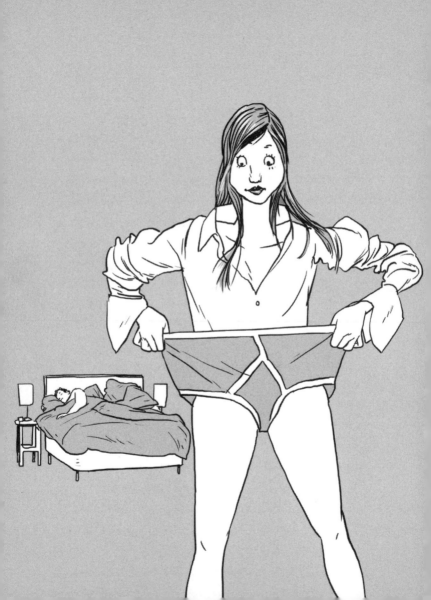

Y-front™ hoarding

There is nothing inherently wrong with a pair of Y-fronts: they offer more support than boxer shorts and are less restrictive than a tight pair of briefs. Not to mention the fact that the majority of the most successful Silicon Valley companies were started by people messing about on computers in nothing but Y-fronts. In many ways they are the perfect pants.

There is, however, something wrong with a pair of Y-fronts that has been living at the back of a man's pants drawer for more than a decade. Once white and pristine, they have grown grey and bitter as newer and brighter undies have taken their place. They are the Miss Havisham of pants and will have their revenge on man by working their way to the front of his drawer whenever a new girlfriend dips in looking for some comfy boyfriend boxers to slip into.

Still, he will not get rid of them ... just in case one day he wakes up and all his other pants have left the country.

Yelling at technology

Smartphones, tablets and self-service devices are designed to make life easier. Yet men who were using trains before the digital revolution yearn for the time when they could buy a ticket from a real, talking human. Instead, unless they want to queue for seventeen hours, they are forced to jab at an unresponsive touchscreen while a line of commuters ponders, often out loud, how anyone could be so perplexed by the simple process of pressing buttons.

In supermarkets these same men can often be found impotently staring at a scan-it-yourself till, wondering why the bagging area finds so much of the produce sold in its own shop unexpected.

A man's default settings aren't calibrated for such technological advances – his reaction to a broken appliance has always been to operate it more vigorously, which is precisely the opposite of what's needed in our brave new world. Continuously pressing 'apply' – even if you do it really hard – only serves to aggravate a frozen webpage. There is no evidence to suggest shouting 'COME ON YOU PIECE OF SHIT' helps either.

Waiting for a screen to thaw is, however, far less painful than dealing with an automated telephone service:

'Please tell me where you are travelling from and to.'

'Ipswich to London Liverpool Street.'

'So that's Penzance to Edinburgh?'

'NO! TWATTING COMPUTER-GENERATED FUCKING IDIOT!'

'Sorry I didn't catch that, did you say Birmingham to St Ives?'

How to use social media

Step 1: Update Facebook with pictures of children, preferably yours, engaging in wholesome activities. Accompany with comments such as: 'Great day out at the farm with my little trooper! He gets cuter every day!'

Step 2: If you don't have children, post images of exotic holidays, glamorous parties or food you are about to eat. Also share links to videos and BuzzFeed articles featuring amusing animals.

Step 3: Remember to apply an Instagram filter to all your photos – Mayfair is reliably flattering.

Step 4: Log in to Twitter and make a satirical quip about current affairs or a politically incendiary comment. Add a hashtag – #PMQs for Prime Minister's Questions, for example – so that interested users who aren't among your followers can find it.

Step 5: Talk about your children sparingly on Twitter. If you must, do it in a tone that clearly indicates they make your life hell: 'The kids are behaving like animals. I'm thinking of taking them to the abattoir.'

Step 6: Go to LinkedIn to celebrate a connection's one-year work anniversary. Try to update your profile regularly – there is a slim chance somebody important might look at it one day.

Step 7: Understand that if you've heard of a social network your teenage children will inevitably have stopped using it.

Youth mimicry

There are men who grow to fear youth as they get older and men who want to replicate it. On balance once a man hits forty arriving to work on a foldable scooter and describing his journey as 'sick' (in a good way) is marginally worse than writing off anybody under twenty not in school uniform or cricket whites as a prison sentence waiting to happen.

'The machine does not isolate man from the great problems of nature but plunges him more deeply into them.'

Antoine de Saint-Exupéry

Z

is for ...

Zany going-out shirts

Men who hit the town in shirts that appear to have been hunted down and savaged by a pack of trigger-happy paintballers also put up signs at work that say: YOU DON'T HAVE TO BE MAD TO WORK HERE ... BUT IT HELPS. And tell strangers whose resting face isn't frozen in a state of constant amusement to: 'Cheer up, it might never happen!'

'Men who consistently leave the toilet seat up secretly want women to get up to go to the bathroom in the middle of the night and fall in.'

Rita Rudner

Zealous but fleeting devotion to new hobbies

By the time a man hits thirty he will have attempted and given up on a string of hobbies and fitness regimes. This will manifest itself in a garage – a small drawer if he lives in London – full of rowing machines, surfboards, half-built go-karts, yoga mats, fishing rods and an array of musical instruments. His smartphone will similarly be crammed to crashing point with apps he downloaded to track his progress and forgot to uninstall when his progress stopped.

He begins each new hobby determined to master its complexities and with a self-confident inkling that, this time, he'll be a natural. It doesn't take long for him to realise he's not a natural and that mastering anything takes hours of practice, which he just can't fit in around work, the pub and all the TV he has on series record.

Zoning out

A man struggles to maintain focus during verbal exchanges that do not revolve around him and his favourite hobbies, especially if there are no pictures involved. He can be told exactly what is happening tomorrow, and what his role is, and yet still, twenty minutes later, ask where the kids are staying and what time they need to be dropped off. Despite this, if you offer to write the details down for him he will point to his head and say: 'Don't worry, it's all in here.'

Zombie apocalypse fantasies

Ask a man how he would handle a plague of zombies and he is likely to have a complex and well-considered answer: he'd put his house on lockdown; identify a local source of food; fashion weapons out of domestic objects and hole up until it was safe to find a location suitable for the rebirth of civilisation.

There are several reasons why the zombie apocalypse appeals to the average man, and why he devotes so much time to fantasising about it. Here are three:

1) He wouldn't have to vacuum.

2) He'd have to live on his survivalist wits. And all men believe their wits are infallible.

3) Most people, including his in-laws and colleagues, could be justifiably disposed of using a pair of garden shears strapped to a broom handle.

He has similar thoughts about alien invasions and nuclear Armageddon. Obviously, when presented with the stark reality of a world without TVs or fridges, most men, apart from a few in America's Deep South, would vote against an apocalypse.

How to kill a zombie

Step 1: Although slow and shambolic, zombies are potentially deadly. If possible, always keep them at more than arm's length from your face.

Step 2: Do not use a gun unless you really have to. Noise attracts the undead. Even the noise of something that might blow its brains out.

Step 3: Arm yourself with a suitable weapon, preferably one that is long and sharp. If you don't have a javelin to hand, simply tie a kitchen knife to one end of a long stick.

Step 4: Take a firm stance, feet shoulder width apart, and wait for the zombie to approach.

Step 5: When it is within range lunge forward, aiming your weapon at one of its eyes.

Step 6: Scramble its brain using a circular motion. Make sure it is completely destroyed; this is the only way to kill a zombie. Once you are convinced it is dead, withdraw your weapon.

Step 6: Look behind you. There's always one behind you.